God:
Existence & Attributes

edited by

Mohammad Ali Shomali

Islamic Reference Series:

Vol. 1   God: Existence & Attributes

Edited by Mohammad Ali Shomali

First published in Great Britain in 2008

ISBN: 9781904934080
1-904-934-08-0

Published by

Institute of Islamic Studies
Islamic Centre of England
140 Maida Vale, London W9 1QB
Tel: (44) 0207 604 5500; Fax: (44) 0207 604 4898
Email: ic-el@ic-el.com

بسم الله الرحمن الرحيم

In the Name of God,
the Most Gracious, the Most Merciful

Table of contents

Introduction

This reference series offers a scholarly introduction to the main aspects of Islamic thought. Bringing together the classic texts and contemporary writings, most of which are being published in English for the first time, each volume provides original and engaging coverage of its subject.

This volume studies the concept of God in Islam. Certainly, God is the most important object of knowledge and the effect that such knowledge can have on one's life cannot be compared to anything else. It is fundamental for those who want to know more about Islam to see how the existence and attributes of God are dealt with in the Islamic scriptures and how they are reflected in the faith and practices of Muslims.

The first paper is entitled "The Image of God in the Qur'an". This paper illustrates that the Qur'anic image of God is personal, that is, God has a personal relationship with every individual. The authors have listed all the names and attributes of God that are mentioned in the Qur'an. In addition to the names that refer directly to the divine essence, like Allah, many divine attributes have also been dealt with in this paper. These have been categorized under the following headings: unity, knowledge, mercifulness and compassion, richness, greatness, thankfulness, power, wisdom, ownership, creatorship, truthfulness, nearness, life and eternity, justice and activeness. This survey shows that the Qur'anic conception of God is a transcendent one: God is the One and nothing is like Him, but at the same time God is very close and immanent. The paper ends with a chart that shows the frequency of these attributes in the Qur'an. For example, it shows that the divine attributes indicating God's mercy and compassion are mentioned five hundred and ninety-eight times in the Qur'an and this is by far the most frequently occurring quality of God in the Qur'an.

The second paper is entitled: "God in Islamic Traditions: A Glance at *Al-Tahwid* by Shaykh al-Saduq". Based on the hadiths from Imam Ali and Imam Rida, this paper tries to present the image of God according to the second most important source of Islam, the Sunnah. All the hadiths in this paper are cited from *Al-Tawhid*, which was compiled by Shaykh al-Saduq in the fourth century. In addition to training great scholars of hadith, Shaykh al-Saduq wrote and compiled about three hundred essays and books, including *Man la Yahduruhu al-Faqih* (For him not in the Presence of a Jurisprudent), which is regarded as the second most important collection of Shi'a hadiths. *Al-Tawhid* consists of sixty-six chapters pertaining to divine essence, attributes and acts.

The third paper is entitled: "The Qur'anic Proof for the Existence of God". This paper is part of the book *God in the Qur'an* by Ayatollah M. H. Beheshti. The author refers to the popular view among the exegetes of the Qur'an that the pagans of the Arab peninsula did not doubt the existence of God, the Creator of the universe. Rather, they only worshipped idols as their "intercessors with God" (10: 18). However, the author personally believes that the view that the Qur'an considers doubt about the existence of God tantamount to doubting a self-evident principle, is not quite justified. It can be understood from some verses of the Qur'an that in this Book, which makes things clear, doubting the very existence of God has not been totally ignored either. The author refers to the story of the Prophet Abraham (6:74-79) and argues that the most noteworthy point in the story that is stressed by Abraham in his consideration of the creatures of this world and their being worthy or unworthy of divinity is that an existent [such as the sun] which is ephemeral and which sets at the end of the day, is a dependent existent, which in itself is a sign of an independent being - its creator and lord. The author goes on to explore the idea of the knowledge of God's existence being innate and the idea of a covenant between man and God (in the world of pre-existence).

The fourth paper is entitled "The Ontological Argument in Islamic Metaphysics". This paper studies the ontological argument or the proof of the truthful as expounded by Ibn Sina and Mulla Sadra and argues that their versions of the argument are more advanced than those developed by their predecessors in the east and west. In this type of argument, the path is the same as that which is intended, that is, existence is demonstrated by existence or the Real by the Real, and the middle term used in this argument is existence itself. The paper concludes that Allamah Tabataba'i's version is the most complete version of the argument and has certain advantages over the other ones, because apart from its conciseness, it relies only upon the absoluteness and eternal necessity of pure existence.

The fifth and final paper is entitled "Divine Justice". Issues such as the meaning and significance of divine justice within the Islamic society, the history of the discussion on divine justice, and different concepts involved in understanding divine justice are dealt with in this paper. The paper ends with the translation of the complete lesson on divine justice ('*adl*) by Ayatollah Misbāh Yazdī (b. 1934) from *The Theological Instructions*.

I would like to thank all who have contributed to this volume and pray for their success in both their personal and academic lives. I should also like to thank Saajida Mehrali for proofreading the entire work. I would particularly like to thank Hujatul-Ilslam wa'l-Muslimin Moezzi, the Director of the Islamic Centre of England, for his support and encouragement. And last, but not the least, I thank God the Almighty for His guidance and favour upon us in the past and present.

Mohammad Ali Shomali
November 2007

The Image of God in the Qur'an

Dr Mohammad Ali Shomali and Mahnaz Heydarpoor

The image of God as presented in the Qur'an is one that speaks of Him in personal terms. God has a personal relationship with every individual. In what follows, we will try to present a detailed account of the attributes of God as portrayed in the Qur'an. Efforts have been made to take every name or attribute of God that is mentioned in the Qur'an into account. Muslims believe that both the meaning and the wording of the Qur'an belong to God and that even slight differences in the letters or the frequency of words are significant. Therefore, divine qualities are given different terms and are separately introduced even though they may look similar. Moreover, the number of times each quality is attributed to God is registered. It must be noted that sometimes the same term may have been applied to beings other than God, so every verse is carefully studied to find the exact number of cases in which a given quality is attributed to Him. When it was grammatically impossible to differentiate a case as related to God or to someone else, the Qur'anic commentaries were consulted and the view that seemed more plausible was followed.

Certainly, this survey is subject to all types of human mistakes and limitations and therefore, it is hoped that other researchers will complete it. For example, future research must also take into account those verses in which information about God is given, but not directly as a name or attribute of God. For example, there are many verbs that are used in the Qur'an for God and they constitute a very important source for understanding the image of God in the Qur'an. The other thing that falls beyond the limits of this paper, but will hopefully be dealt with by others, is an elaboration of the concepts attributed to God. For example, when we talk about divine knowledge or divine mercy there are many more details to be learnt from the Qur'an about their nature and functions.

There are different ways of classifying the divine attributes among Muslim theologians. For example, one way of classification is to divide them into the attributes of beauty (*jamāl*) and glory (*jalāl*). The former includes those attributes that indicate divine perfections in an affirmative way, such as knowledge, mercy and power. These attributes are also called, "*al-ṣifāt al-thubūtiyyah*" (the Affirmative Attributes). The latter includes those attributes that describe God in a negative way, that is, by indicating divine freedom from imperfections and deficiencies. Examples are that God is not a body and has no place, God has no part or partner and He neither begets nor is he begotten. The other way of classifying divine attributes is to divide them into the attributes of essence and action. Attributes of essence (*al-ṣifāt al-dhātiyyah*) are those attributes that describe divine essence and do not depend on any being other than God Himself, such as power and life. Attributes relating to action (*al-ṣifāt al-fiʿliyyah*) are those attributes that describe divine acts and, indeed, inform us of a relationship between God and other beings. For example, divine creatorship describes a very specific relationship between God and His creatures. This attribute becomes actual when there is something that is created by God. Another example is forgiveness. There must be someone who is forgiven for us to be able to say that God has forgiven. Of course, to create or to forgive depends on certain essential qualities of God.

In what follows, we will try to avoid sophisticated theological discussions and instead, will just classify divine names and attributes that are mentioned in the Qur'an according to their similarities.

Allāh, Ilāh and Rabb

Allāh (الله): This is the main name for God in the Qur'an. Indeed, this is the main name of God in Arabic used by Muslims and non-

Muslims alike. For example, in an Arabic edition of the Bible, the word 'Allah' is used for God. In the Qur'an, Allah is mentioned 2816 times (including its variations such as *lillāh, tallāh, billāh* and *Allāhuma*). There are different views about the origin of this term. The most plausible view seems to be that it is the abbreviated form of *al-ilāh*. In Arabic, *al-* is the definite article and *ilāh* means god. To be more precise, ilāh is derived from the root *"a-la-ha"*, which means 'worship'. Thus, ilāh means what is worshipped or worthy of being worshipped, just like *kitāb*, which means what is written or what can be written. The standard formulation of faith in Islam involves the declaration of two facts: *Lā ILāHA ILLALLāH and MUHAMMADUR- RASŪLULLāH* (There is no god but God and Muhammad is His messenger). As indicated in the Qur'an, it is clear that there have always been false gods. So when it is said, 'There is no god but God' it is obvious that it means, 'There is no real god or no one worthy of worship but God'.

Ilāh (اله): This is mentioned 120 times. In 37 cases, it is used for false gods. In the rest, it is either used for God specifically or in the general sense. For example, the Qur'an says:

> "Were you witnesses when death approached Jacob, when he said to his children, 'What will you worship after me?' They said, 'We will worship your god (God), and the god (God) of your fathers, Abraham, Ishmael, and Isaac, the one god (One God), and to Him do we submit.'" (2:133)

and

> "Your god (God) is the one god (One God), there is no god except Him, the All-beneficent, the All-merciful." (2:163)

Rabb (رب): In Arabic, the term *rabb* means lord. It is mostly used for God, but it may also be used in a broader sense to be synonymous with master, guardian or owner. In the Qur'an, this

13

term has been used for God 963 times. This shows the utmost importance of this quality of God. The only word that is used more frequently to denote God in the Qur'an is Allah.

Divine Attributes

1. Unity: The Unity of God is one of the most important principles of Islam. Although the Qur'an sometimes speaks about and presents arguments about the existence of God, the main emphasis of the Qur'an is put on the attributes of God, especially His unity and mercy. The Qur'an considers the existence of God to be a very obvious fact, whose acknowledgement requires more straightforward contemplation than complicated philosophical arguments. Even the pagans believed in God, but they were polytheists in the sense that they associated partners with God and worshipped idols. They did not however, deny the existence of God the Creator, and even argued that the idols were a means to reach him, saying, "We do not worship them [idols] except for them taking us closer to God". The idea of the unity of God is asserted in many different ways. Among them, are two attributes that explicitly indicate His oneness:

1.1. Wāhid (واحد): Literally meaning "one". This is applied to God 21 times in the Qur'an, such as in the following verse:

> "Your god is the One God, there is no god except Him, the All-beneficent, the All-merciful." (2:163)

1.2. Ahad (احد): Literally meaning "one". This is applied to God once, in the verse below. The difference between Ahad and Wahid is that the former is used for something that is one and at the same time indivisible, something that has neither partner nor part.

> "Say, 'He is God, the One." (112:1)

2. Knowledge: One of the common qualities of God among followers of the Abrahamic faiths is knowledge. In Judaism,

14

Christianity and Islam, God is thought of as the 'Omniscient', indicating that He has all the knowledge. There are hundreds of verses in which the Qur'an talks about different aspects of divine knowledge. The reason for this emphasis lies partly in the great impact that belief in such an idea may have on people's lives. When we remember that the world is created and run by God who knows everything and that whatever we do or believe, or even intend, is known by Him and that He is fully aware of our needs, sufferings, interests, limits and capabilities, our attitude to the world and to our lives becomes totally different. What follows is a detailed look at the occurrences of this quality of the knowledge of God in the Qur'an:

2.1. **'Alīm (علیم):** Meaning the All-Knowing or the Omniscient. This attribute is used for God in the Qur'an 153 times. One example is in the following verse of the Qur'an:

"Ah! You are the ones who bear love towards them, while they do not love you, though you believe in all the Books; and when they meet you, they say, 'We believe', but when they are alone, they bite their fingertips out of rage at you. Say, 'Die of your rage!' Indeed, God is **All-knowing** of what is in the breasts." (3:119)

2.2. **A'lam (اعلم):** Meaning the Best Knower or the Most-Knowing. This attribute of God is mentioned in the Qur'an 48 times. For example, the Qur'an says:

"Your Lord is **the Best Knower** of whoever is in the heavens and the earth. Certainly We gave some prophets an advantage over others, and We gave David the Psalms." (17:55)

2.3. **Baṣīr (بصیر):** Meaning the All Seeing or the Seer, this is attributed to God 42 times. For example, the Qur'an says:

"Your relatives and your children will not benefit you on the Day of Resurrection: He will separate you [from one another], and God is **the Seer** of what you do." (60:3)

2.4. **Samī' (سميع):** Meaning the All Hearing. This quality of God is mentioned 46 times in the Qur'an. One instance is quoted below:

"Say, 'If I go astray, my going astray is only to my own harm, and if I am rightly guided that is because of what my Lord has revealed to me. Indeed He is **All-hearing**, nearmost.'" (34:50)

2.5. **Khabīr (خبير):** Literally meaning well aware. This attribute is used 45 times in the Qur'an for God:

"So have faith in God and His Apostle and the light which We have sent down, and God is **well aware** of what you do." (64:8)

2.6. **Laṭīf (لطيف):** Meaning attentive and/or subtle (or knower of subtleties). This is attributed to God seven times in the Qur'an. For example, the Qur'an says:

"Have you not regarded that Allah sends sown water from the sky, whereupon the earth turns green? Indeed Allah is **All-attentive [and/or subtle or knower of subtleties]**, all-aware." (22:63)

2.7. **Raqīb (رقيب):** Literally meaning the Watchful. This is used for God 4 times in the Qur'an. One of the four verses in which it is used is quoted here:

"O mankind! Be wary of your Lord who created you from a single soul, and created its mate from it, and, from the two of them, scattered numerous men and women. Be wary of God, in whose Name you adjure one another, and the wombs. Indeed God is **Watchful** over you." (4:1)

2.8. **Qā'im (قائم):** Literally meaning standing. This is used once in the Qur'an to denote the watchful quality of God:

"Is He who is **Watchful** over every soul as to what it earns [comparable to the idols]? And yet they ascribe partners to Allah..." (13:33)

2.9. **'Allām al-ghuyūb (علام الغيوب):** Literally meaning the Knower of all that is Unseen. This is mentioned 4 times in the Qur'an, such as in the following verse:

"The day God will gather the apostles and say, 'What was the response to you?' They will say, 'We have no knowledge. Indeed You are **Knower of all that is Unseen.**'" (5:109)

2.10. **'Ālim al-ghayb wa al-shahādah (عالم الغيب والشهاده):** Literally meaning Knower of the Unseen and the Sensible. This is mentioned 10 times in the Qur'an. One example is:

"That is **the Knower of the Sensible and the Unseen**, the All-mighty, the All-merciful." (32:6)

2.11. **'Ālim al-ghayb (عالم الغيب):** Literally meaning the Knower of the Unseen. This is mentioned 3 times: twice in a general way and once in respect to the heavens and the earth. The following are examples of how the quality is used in various verses:

"Knower of the Unseen, He does not disclose His Unseen to anyone, except to an apostle He approves of. Then He dispatches a sentinel before and behind him so that He may ascertain that they have communicated the messages of their Lord, and He comprehends all that is with them, and He keeps count of all things." (72:26 -28)

and

> "Indeed God is **the Knower of the Unseen of the heavens and the earth**. Indeed He knows well what is in the breasts." (35:38)

2.12. God is not **ghāfil** (غافل), that is, oblivious or unmindful. This idea is mentioned 11 times in the Qur'an, like in the following instance:

> "Certainly We created above you the seven tiers and We have **not** been **oblivious** of creation." (23:17)

2.13. God is not **nasiyy** (نسى), that is, forgetful. This idea is mentioned once in the Qur'an in the following verse:

> "We do not descend except by the command of your Lord. To Him belongs whatever is before us and whatever is behind us and whatever is in between that, and your Lord is **not forgetful**." (19:64)

3. Mercifulness and compassion: After the unity of God, the mercy and compassion of God seems to be the most important aspect of the Qur'anic image of Him. There are more attributes in this category than any other category and altogether they are by far the most often repeated characteristics of God in the Qur'an. Every chapter of the Qur'an starts with بسم الله الرحمن الرحيم except Chapter 9. However, Chapter 27 contains this phrase twice: once in the beginning and then again in the verse 27:30. In such an extraordinarily important phrase which stands as a symbol for Islam and occurs 114 times in the Qur'an and with which Muslims are highly recommended to begin every act or speech, two attributes in particular are singled out: al-Rahman and al-Rahim. Another interesting case is the first chapter of the Qur'an, the Opening, which has seven verses. Indeed, this chapter is a brief account of Islam, without which no ritual prayer can be performed. The chapter starts with the phrase بسم الله الرحمن الرحيم as usual, but then proceeds as follows:

"All praise belongs to God, Lord of all the worlds, the All-compassionate, the All-merciful, Master of the Day of Retribution. You [alone] do we worship, and to You [alone] do we turn for help. Guide us on the straight path, the path of those whom You have blessed, not the path of those who have incurred Your wrath, nor are astray." (2:2-7)

As we see, in this important chapter four attributes of God are mentioned: the Lord of all the worlds, the All-compassionate, the All-merciful and Master of the Day of Retribution. These four must be very significant and therefore they deserve careful study In brief, they refer to two acts of God: the first is that He is the one who runs the universe and the second is that He is the one who establishes justice. They also refer to two qualities of God: the All-compassionate and the All-merciful. This indicates that the primary factors and governing principles in the entire creation are divine compassion and mercy. In the following discussion, the different divine names and qualities that indicate God's mercy will be explained in some detail.

3.1. **Al-Rahmān** (الرحمـان): Literally meaning the All-compassionate or the All-merciful. This is the second most famous name of God in Islam. In the Qur'an God tells the Prophet Mohammad:

> "Say, 'Invoke "Allah" or invoke "**al-Rahmān**." Whichever [of His Names] you may invoke, to Him belong the Best Names.'" (17:110)

This term is mentioned 169 times in the Qur'an.

3.2. **Al-Rahīm** (رحيم): Literally meaning the Compassionate or the Merciful. It is the most repeated attribute of God in the Qur'an. It is mentioned 226 times in the Qur'an. According to some hadiths, Al-Rahman refers to the compassion and mercy of God for all creatures and al-Rahim refers to the special extra compassion and mercy that He has for the believers. Thus, it may

19

be more accurate to translate al-Rahman into the All-merciful and al-Rahim into the Most merciful

> "Then indeed your Lord, to those who commit evil out of ignorance and then repent after that, and reform - indeed, after that, your Lord will surely be All-forgiving, **All-merciful**." (16:119)

3.3. **Arham al-rāhimīn** (ارحم الراحمين): Literally meaning the most merciful of the merciful ones. This is attributed to God four times in the Qur'an. One of these instances is mentioned below:

> "And Job, when he called out to his Lord, 'Indeed distress has befallen me, and You are **the Most merciful of the merciful**.'" (21:83)

3.4. **Khayr al-rāhimīn** (خيرالراحمين): Literally meaning the best of those who are merciful. This has occurred twice in the Qur'an for God, such as in the following verse:

> "Say, 'My Lord, forgive and have mercy, and You are **the Best of those who are merciful**.'" (23:118)

3.5. **Dhu al-rahmah** (ذوالرحمة): Literally meaning the possessor or the dispenser of mercy. This is used for God twice. One of these verses is:

> "Your Lord is the All-forgiving **Possessor of mercy**. Were He to take them to task because of what they have committed, He would have surely hastened their punishment. But they have a tryst, [when] they will not find a refuge besides Him." (18:58)

3.6. **Dhū rahmat-in wāsi'ah** (ذو رحمة واسعه): Literally meaning the possessor of an embracing mercy or the dispenser of all-embracing mercy, this is used for God once in the Qur'an in the following verse:

"But if they deny you, say, 'Your Lord is **Possessor of an all-embracing mercy**, but His punishment will not be averted from the guilty lot.'" (6:147)

3.7. **Wadūd** (ودود)**:** Literally meaning Affectionate. This divine attribute is mentioned twice in the Qur'an. One instance is in the verse below:

"Plead with your Lord for forgiveness, then turn to Him penitently. My Lord is indeed All-merciful, **All-affectionate.**'" (11:90)

3.8. **Al-Akram** (الاكرم)**:** Literally meaning the most generous. This is used for God once in the Qur'an:

"Read, and your Lord is **the Most generous**, who taught by the pen, taught man what he did not know." (96:3-5)

3.9. **Khayr-un thawāb-an** (خير ثوابا)**:** Literally meaning the best in rewarding. This is used once in the Qur'an:

"There all guardianship belongs to God, the Real. He is **Best in rewarding**, and Best giver of success." (18:44)

3.10. **Ghaffār** (غفار)**:** Meaning all-forgiver. This is applied to God five times, like in the following verse:

"...telling [them]: 'Plead to your Lord for forgiveness. Indeed He is **All-forgiver.**'" (71:10)

3.11. **Ahl al-maghfirah** (اهل المغفرة)**:** Meaning the one who is worthy or qualified to forgive. This is applied to God once, in the verse below:

"And they will not remember unless God wishes. He is worthy of [your] being wary [of Him] and He is **Worthy to forgive**." (74:56)

3.12. Wāsiʿ al-maghfirah (واسع المغفره): Meaning expansive in forgiveness. This is attributed to God once in the following verse:

"Those who avoid major sins and indecencies, excepting [minor and occasional] lapses. Indeed your Lord is **Expansive in [His] forgiveness**. He knows you best since [the time] He produced you from the earth, and since you were foetuses in the bellies of your mothers. So do not flaunt your piety: He knows best those who are wary of God." (53:32)

3.13. Khayr al-ghāfirīn (خير الغافرين): Meaning the best of those who forgive. This is used once, in the verse given below:

"Moses chose seventy men from his people for Our tryst, and when the earthquake seized them, he said, 'My Lord, had You wished, You would have destroyed them and me before. Will You destroy us because of what the fools amongst us have done? It is only Your test by which You lead astray whomever You wish and guide whomever You wish. You are our master, so forgive us and have mercy on us, for You are **the Best of those who forgive**." (7:155)

3.14. Karīm (كريم): Meaning generous. This divine attribute is mentioned twice in the Qur'an. One of these occasions is in the following verse:

"O Man! What has deceived you about your **Generous** Lord, who created you and proportioned you, and gave you an upright nature, and composed you in any form that He wished?" (82:6-8)

3.15. **Ghāfir al-dhanb** (غافرالذنب): Meaning forgiver of sins. This is mentioned once in the Qur'an in the following verse:

"**Forgiver of sins** and Acceptor of repentance, Severe in retribution, [yet] All-bountiful, there is no god except Him, [and] toward Him is the destination." (40:3)

3.16. **Qābil al-Tawb** (قابل التوب): Meaning acceptor of repentance. This is mentioned once in verse 40:3, mentioned above.

3.17. **Dhi al-ṭawl** (ذى الطول): Meaning the Bountiful. This is mentioned once in verse 40:3 above.

3.18. **Dhu al-jalāl wa al-ikrām** (ذو الجلال و الاكرام): Meaning the one who has majesty and generosity. This is mentioned twice in the Qur'an, once for God Himself and on another occasion, for His face (*wajh*). For example, the Qur'an says:

"Blessed is the Name of your Lord, **Possessor of majesty and generosity!**" (55:78)

Here, a combination of two qualities is presented, generosity and majesty. The former is related to the mercy of god and the second will be explained later.

3.19. **Tawwāb** (تواب): Tawbah literally means return. When it is used for human beings it means repentance. When someone repents it means that he is returning back to God and is trying to restore his relation with God, which was affected and/or harmed as a result of his sins. However, the Qur'an speaks of God's return as well. According to the Qur'an, our repentance is surrounded by two 'returns' from God. As for a sinful person whose relation with God is damaged, it is God Himself who first initiates reconciliation by inviting His servant to return and by making his heart soft. Then after the servant feels really remorseful and repents, God the Almighty embraces him with mercy and forgives him. This quality is mentioned 11 times in the Qur'an. One of these times is mentioned below:

> "…and to the three who were left behind. When the earth became narrow for them with [all] its expanse, and their own souls weighed heavily on them, and they knew that there was no refuge from God except in Him, then He returned toward them so that they might repent. Indeed God is **Oft-returning**, the All-merciful." (9:118)

3.20. **Dhu al-fadl al-'azīm (ذوالفضل العظيم):** Meaning the possessor of great grace. This is mentioned in the Qur'an for God 13 times, such as in the following example:

> "O you who have faith! If you are wary of God, He shall appoint a criterion for you (to judge between right and wrong), and absolve you of your misdeeds, and forgive you, for God is **Possessor of great grace**." (8:29)

3.21. **Ra'ūf (رؤوف):** Literally meaning very kind. This is mentioned for God ten times in the Qur'an. One instance is mentioned below:

> "It is He who sends down manifest signs to His servant that He may bring you out of darkness into light, and indeed God is **Most kind** and Most merciful to you." (57:9)

3.22. **Ghafūr (غفور):** Meaning oft-forgiving. This is mentioned 91 times in the Qur'an. For example, the Qur'an says:

> "When those who have faith in Our signs come to you, say, 'Peace to you! Your Lord has made mercy incumbent upon Himself: whoever of you commits an evil [deed] out of ignorance and then repents after that

and reforms, then He is indeed **Oft-forgiving**, Most merciful.'" (6:54)

3.23. **Halīm (حليم):** Meaning all-forbearing. This quality of God is mentioned 11 times in the Qur'an. One of the verses that demonstrates this is:

> "The seven heavens glorify Him, and the earth [too], and whoever is in them. There is not a thing but celebrates His praise, but you do not understand their glorification. Indeed He is **All-forbearing**, Oft-forgiving." (17:44)

3.24. **Wahhāb (وهاب):** Meaning the one who bestows many blessings or the one who is very munificent. This is applied to God three times in the Qur'an, such as in the following verse:

> "[They say,] 'Our Lord! Do not make our hearts swerve after You have guided us, and bestow Your mercy on us. Indeed You are the **All-munificent**." (3:8)

3.25. **'Afuww (عفو):** Meaning all-pardoning or all-excusing. This is mentioned as a quality of God five times. One example is given below:

> "Whether you disclose a good [deed that you do] or hide it, or excuse an evil [deed], God is indeed **All-excusing**, All-powerful." (4:149)

3.26. **Mujīb (مجيب):** Meaning responsive. This is mentioned once for God, in the following verse:

> "And to Thamud [We sent] Salih, their brother. He said, 'O my people! Worship God. You have no other god besides Him. He brought you forth from the earth and made it your habitation. So plead with Him for

forgiveness, then turn to Him penitently. My Lord is indeed Nearmost [and] **Responsive**.'" (11:61)

3.27. **Dhu maghfirah (ذومغفرة):** Meaning the one who has (the habit of) forgiveness. This is mentioned twice in the Qur'an:

"Nothing is said to you except what has already been said [earlier] to the apostles before you. Indeed your Lord is Forgiving and One who metes out a painful retribution." (41:43)

3.28. **Hamīd (حميد):** Meaning praised or praiseworthy. This is applied to God 17 times in the Qur'an. The following verse is one example:

"O mankind! You are the ones who stand in need of God, and God - He is the All-sufficient, the **All-praiseworthy**." (35:15)

3.29. **Khayr (خير):** Meaning better, this is applied to God three times in the Qur'an. One instance is mentioned below:

"We have indeed believed in our Lord that He may forgive us our iniquities and the magic you compelled us to perform. Allah is **Better** and More lasting." (20:73)

3.30. **Barr (بر):** Meaning benign. This is applied to God once:

"...indeed we used to supplicate Him aforetime. Indeed He is the **All-benign**, the All-merciful." (52:28)

3.31. **Nūr (نور):** Meaning light. This is used for God once and that is in the well-known verse of the Light which reads as follows:

"God is the **Light** of the heavens and the earth. The parable of His Light is a niche wherein is a lamp - the lamp is in a glass, the glass as it were a glittering star - lit from a blessed olive tree, neither eastern nor western, whose oil almost lights up, though fire should not touch it. Light upon light. God guides to His Light whomever He wishes. God draws parables for mankind, and God has knowledge of all things." (24:35)

3.32. **Salām (سلام):** Meaning peace or source of peace. This is mentioned as a divine quality once:

"He is Allah there is no god except Him the Sovereign, the All-holy, the **Source of peace**, the Securer, the All-compeller, the All-magnanimous. Clear is Allah of any partners that they may ascribe [to Him]!" (59:23)

3.33. **Quddūs (قدوس):** Meaning holy. This is applied to God twice in the Qur'an, like in the following verse:

"Whatever there is in the heavens glorifies Allah and whatever there is in the earth, the Sovereign, the **All-holy**, the All-mighty, the All-wise." (62:1)

3.34. **Khayr al-wārithīn (خير الوارثين):** Meaning the best of inheritors. This is mentioned as a divine quality once:

"And Zechariah, when he cried out to his Lord, 'My Lord! Do not leave me without an heir, and You are the **Best of inheritors.**'" (21:89)

3.35. **Khayr-un 'uqbā (خير عقبى):** Literally meaning best in end. This is used once in the Qur'an for God in the sense that He is the Best giver of success. The Qur'an says:

"There, the (only) protection comes from Allah, the True One. He is the Best to reward, and **the Best giver of success.**" (18:44)

4. Richness: According to the Qur'an, God is rich and free from any kind of need. Everything else is a creation of God and entirely dependent on him.

4.1. **Ghaniyy (غنى):** Meaning rich. This is used as a divine quality 18 times, such as in the following verse:

> "Certainly We gave Luqman wisdom, saying, 'Give thanks to God; and whoever gives thanks, gives thanks only for his own sake. And whoever is ungrateful, [let him know that] God is indeed **Rich**, All-praiseworthy.'" (31:12)

4.2. **Ṣamad (صمد):** Literally meaning self-sufficient or impregnable. This is attributed to God once, in the following verse:

> "Say, 'He is God, the One. God is **the Self-sufficient**. He neither gave birth, nor was he begotten, nor has He any equal.'" (112:1-3)

5. Greatness: According to the Qur'an, God is great in all aspects of perfection. Indeed, His greatness exceeds all measurement and calculation. This is why Muslim thinkers tend not to compare anything with God in greatness, even by saying something like, "God is greater than us or than the universe". It is because of this that the well-known Islamic invocation and motto, "Allah-u Akbar" is interpreted in hadith as meaning "God is greater than any being described (or characterized)".

5.1. **Wāsiʿ (واسع):** Literally meaning All-encompassing. This is mentioned as a divine quality eight times in the Qur'an. One example is as follows:

> "To God belongs the East and the West: so whichever way you turn, there is the face of God! God is indeed **All-encompassing**, All-knowing." (2:115)

5.2. **'Azīz (عزيز):** Meaning the Almighty. This is mentioned as a divine quality 90 times in the Qur'an. An example is:

> "And put your trust in the **Almighty**, the All-merciful." (26:217)

5.3. **'Aliyy (على):** Meaning most high or exalted. This divine quality is mentioned eight times in the Qur'an, such as when Allah says:

> "To Him belongs whatever is in the heavens and whatever is in the earth, and He is the **Exalted**, the Supreme." (42:4)

5.4. **'Azīm (عظيم):** Meaning great or supreme. This divine quality is mentioned six times in the Qur'an. For instance, when Allah says:

> "So celebrate the Name of your Lord, the **supreme**." (56:74 & 96)

5.5. **Kabīr (كبير):** This also denotes the meaning great or supreme. It is mentioned as a divine quality six times in the Qur'an:

> "That is because God is the Reality, and whatever they invoke besides Him is nullity, and because God is the All-exalted, the **Great**." (31:30 & 22:62)

5.6. **Majīd (مجيد):** Meaning All-glorious. This is used twice for God in the Qur'an. For example,

> "They said, 'Are you amazed at God's dispensation? [That is] God's mercy and His blessings upon you, members of the household. Indeed He is All-praiseworthy, **the Glorious**.'" (11:73)

5.7. **Muta'āl (متعال):** Meaning the Exalted. This is used for God once in the following verse of the Holy Qur'an:

> "…the Knower of the sensible and the Unseen, the Great, the **Exalted**." (13:9)

5.8. **A'lā (اعلىٰ):** Meaning the most high or the Exalted, this is used as a divine quality twice in the Qur'an, such as in the following verse:

> "…but seeks only the pleasure of his Lord, the **Most Exalted.**" (92:20)

5.9. **Rafī' al-darajāt (رفيع الدرجات):** Meaning raiser of ranks or raised high above ranks. This is mentioned for God once, in the following verse:

> "**Raiser of ranks**, Lord of the Throne, He casts the Spirit of His command upon whomever of His servants that He wishes, that he may warn [people] of the Day of Encounter." (40:15)

5.10. **Dhu al-'Arsh (ذوالعرش):** Meaning the possessor of the Throne. This is applied to God four times in the Qur'an. An example is:

> "Possessor of the Throne, the All-glorious." (85:15)

5.11. **Dhu al-jalāl (ذو الجلال):** Meaning the one who has majesty. As said above in 3.18, this is mentioned twice in the Qur'an: once for God Himself and another time for His face (*wajh*). For example, the Qur'an says:

> "Blessed is the Name of your Lord, the **Possessor of majesty** and generosity!" (55:78)

5.12. **Muhīṭ (محيط):** Meaning encompassing or comprehensive, this is attributed to God eight times in the Qur'an, like in the verse:

> "To Allah belongs whatever is in the heavens and whatever is on the earth, and Allah is **All-encompassing** (or **comprehends** all things)." (4:126)

5.13. **Mutakabbir (متكبر):** Meaning the Magnanimous, this is used as a divine quality just once in the Holy Qur'an, in the following verse:

> "He is God, there is no god except Him, the Sovereign, the All-holy, the All-benign, the Securer, the All-conserver, the Almighty, the All-compeller, the **Magnanimous**. Clear is God of any partners that they may ascribe [to Him]!" (59:23)

5.14. **Dhi al-maʿārij (ذى المعارج):** Meaning the one who possesses the tools of ascent. This is used for God once in the following verse:

> "...from God, **Possessor** of the Ways of Ascent." (70:3)

6. Thankfulness: Normally people think that thankfulness is a virtue for human beings. When granted some help or gift or the like, human beings feel obliged and render their gratitude to the giver. However, the Qur'an tells us that thankfulness is also one of the qualities of God. Although everything that we humans have belongs to God the Almighty, He appreciates even the little good acts that we perform and thanks us. This idea is addressed by considering the following qualities of God.

6.1. **Shākir (شاكر):** Meaning thankful or appreciative. This is mentioned as a divine quality twice. One of these is mentioned below:

"Indeed Safa and Marwah are among God's sacraments. So whoever makes hajj to the House, or performs the 'umrah, then there is no sin on him to circuit between them. Should anyone do good of his own accord, then God is indeed **Appreciative**, All-knowing." (2:158)

6.2. **Shakūr** (شكور)**:** Meaning very thankful or appreciative. This is mentioned as a divine quality four times in the Holy Qur'an. One of these examples is below:

"…that He may pay them their reward in full and enhance them out of His grace. Indeed He is All-forgiving, **Appreciative**." (35:30)

7. Power: One qualities of God that is common among followers of the Abrahamic faiths, is power. In Judaism, Christianity and Islam, God is known as the 'Omnipotent', indicating that He has all the power and is capable of doing anything. The Qur'an emphasises this fact by using the following attributes for God:

7.1. **Qadīr** (قدير)**:** Meaning very powerful, this is used in the Qur'an for God 45 times, such as in the following instance:

"Blessed is He in whose hands is all sovereignty, and He is **powerful** over all things." (67:1)

7.2. **Ashadd-u quwwat-an** (اشد قوة)**:** Meaning more powerful and is mentioned only once:

"As for [the people of] 'Ad, they acted arrogantly in the earth unduly, and they said, 'Who is more powerful than us?' Did they not see that Allah, who created them, is **more powerful** than them?" (41:15)[1]

7.3. **Qāhir** (قاهر)**:** Meaning the dominant or the absolute. This is mentioned as a divine quality of God twice in the Holy Qur'an, as shown in the example below:

"He is the **All-dominant** over His servants, and He sends guards to [protect] you. When death approaches anyone of you, Our messengers take him away and they do not neglect [their duty]." (6:61)

7.4. **Qādir** (قادر): Meaning able or powerful. This is mentioned seven times. One example is:

"Do they not see that God, who created the heavens and the earth and [who] was not exhausted by their creation, is able to revive the dead? Yes, indeed He is **powerful** over all things." (46:33)

7.5. **Qādirūn** (قادرون): This is the plural form of Qādir and is used for God five times. When God talks about Himself or His acts in the Holy Qur'an, He often uses the plural form to indicate His most high position. This can be compared to the way in which monarchies are often referred to or addressed by using plural form. Some people have suggested that another reason for using the plural form in the Qur'an is that God normally does things through His agents, and therefore His acts are, in a sense, a collective enterprise. Interestingly, unlike popular usage, God is never addressed in the Qur'an and hadiths in a plural form. This is to put utmost emphasis on the unity of God and the fact that it is only Him who can be worshiped. One of the verses in which the quality of being powerful is used for God in the plural form is the following:

"Does man suppose that We shall not put together his bones? Yes indeed, We are **Able** to proportion [even] his fingertips! Rather man desires to go on living viciously." (75:3-5)

7.6. **Qawiyy** (قوى): This means powerful or strong and is used nine times for God in the Qur'an. One example is:

"God is All-attentive to His servants. He provides for whomever He wishes, and He is the **Strong**, the All-mighty." (42:19)

7.7. Hafīz (حفيظ): Meaning preserver or protector. This is used for God three times. One of these is in the following verse:

"But if you turn your backs [on me], then [know that] I have communicated to you whatever I was sent to you with. My Lord will make another people succeed you, and you will not hurt God in the least. Indeed my Lord is **Preserver** of [and **Watchful**] over all things." (11:57)

7.8. Ghālib-un 'alā 'amrih (غالب على امره): Meaning master of his affair. This quality is used once in the Qur'an for God. It denotes that God has full command of His affairs and whatever He decides will certainly happen. The Qur'an says:

"The man from Egypt who had bought him [Joseph] said to his wife, 'Give him an honourable place [in the household]. Maybe he will be useful to us, or we may adopt him as a son.' Thus We established Joseph in the land that We might teach him the interpretation of dreams. God is **Master of His affairs**, but most people do not know." (12:21)

7.9. Hāfizīn (حافظين): This is the plural form of Hāfiz, which means the preserver, protector or guardian and is used for God twice. For example, the Qur'an says:

"Indeed We have sent down the Reminder, and We will most surely be its guardian." (15:9)

7.10. Qahhār (قهار): Meaning very dominant and absolute or paramount. This is used as a divine quality six times in the Qur'an. One example is:

"The day the earth is transformed into another earth and the heavens [as well], and they are presented before God, the One, the **All-dominant**." (14:48)

7.11. **Khayr-un hāfizan** (خير حافظا): Meaning the best protector. This is mentioned once in the Qur'an for God, in the following verse:

"He said, 'Should I trust you with him just as I trusted you with his brother before?' Yet God is **the Best protector**, and He is the most merciful of merciful ones." (12:64)

7.12. **Shadid al-mihāl** (شديد المحال): Meaning great in might. This is mentioned as a divine quality once in the Qur'an:

"The Thunder celebrates His praise, and the angels [too], in awe of Him, and He releases the thunderbolts and strikes with them whomever He wishes. Yet they dispute concerning God, though He is **Great in might**." (13:13)

7.13. **Muqtadir** (مقتدر): Meaning (very) powerful. This is mentioned three times in the Qur'an for God, like in the verse:

"Draw for them the parable of the life of this world: [It is] like the water We send down from the sky. Then the earth's vegetation mingles with it. Then it becomes chaff, scattered by the wind. And God is **Powerful** over all things." (18:45)

7.14. **Muqtadirūn** (مقتدرون): This is the plural form of Muqdtadir and is used once in the Qur'an for God:

"We shall show you what We have promised them, for indeed We are the **Possessors of full power** over them." (43:42)

7.15. Dhu al-Quwwah (ذوالقوة): Meaning the possessor of power or the powerful. This is used once in the following verse:

"Indeed it is God who is the All-provider, **Powerful**, All-strong." (51:58)

7.16. Matin (متين): This means strong or firm and is mentioned as a divine quality once:

"Indeed it is Allah who is the All-provider, Powerful, **All-strong**." (51:58)

7.17. Muhaymin (مهيمن): Meaning guardian or conserver. This is mentioned as a divine quality just once:

"He is God, there is no god except Him, the Sovereign, the All-holy, the All-benign, the Securer, **the All-conserver**, the All-mighty, the All-compeller, the All-magnanimous. Clear is God of any partners that they may ascribe [to Him]!" (59:23)

7.18. Jabbār (جبار): Meaning all-compeller. This is mentioned as a divine quality just once in the verse 59:23.

7.19. Muqīt (مقيت): Meaning powerful and preserver. This is mentioned as a divine quality in the following verse:

"Whoever intercedes for a good cause shall receive a share of it, and whoever intercedes for an evil cause shall share its burden, and Allah is **Powerful** over all things." (4:85)

7.20. Ashadd-u ba's-an (اشد بأسا): Meaning greater or greatest in power and might. This has been attributed to God once:

"So fight in the way of Allah: you are responsible only for yourself, but urge on the faithful [to fight]. Maybe Allah will curb the might of the faithless, for

36

Allah is **Greatest in might** and Severest in punishment." (4:84)

7.21. God does not take as His aid those who mislead. This is mentioned once in the Qur'an:

> "I did not make them a witness to the creation of the heavens and the earth, nor to their own creation, nor do I take those who mislead as assistants." (18:51)

7.22. God is never outrun or outmanoeuvred. This is mentioned twice. One example is:

> "We have ordained death among you, and We are not to be outmanoeuvred." (56:60)

8. **Wisdom:** According to the Qur'an God is the Wise (*hakim*). God never does anything in vain. This attribute of God is mentioned 91 times, such as in the following verse:

> "O Moses! Indeed I am Allah, the All-mighty, **the Wise**." (27:9)

9. Ownership

9.1. **Mālik (مالک):** Meaning owner or master, this is used twice for God in the Holy Qur'an. One of the verses where it is used is:

> "**Master** of the Day of Retribution." (1:4)

9.2. **Malik (ملک):** Meaning king or sovereign, this is used as a divine quality five times in the Qur'an. For example:

> "So exalted is Allah, the True **Sovereign**. There is no god except Him, the Lord of the Noble Throne." (23:116)

9.3. **Malīk (ملیک):** Meaning king or sovereign, this is used once in the Qur'an as a divine quality:

"...in the abode of truthfulness with a Powerful **King**." (54:55)

10. Creatorship: The idea that God is the creator of the world is mentioned in hundreds of Qur'anic verses. However, in most of the cases instead of names or adjectives, verbs are used. As mentioned in the beginning, here we will just refer to those cases in which a name or adjective that refers to the creative ability of God is used.

10.1. Badī' (بديع): Meaning creator or originator. God is introduced as the creator of the heavens and the earth, twice, like in the following example:

"...the **Originator** of the heavens and the earth; and when He decides on a matter, He just says to it, 'Be!' and it is." (2:117)

10.2. Fāṭir (فاطر): Meaning creator or originator. This is mentioned six times:

"The originator of the heavens and the earth, He made for you mates from your own selves, and mates of the cattle, by which means He multiplies you. Nothing is like Him. And He is the All-hearing, the All-seeing." (42:11)

10.3. Fāliq al-habb wa al-nawā (فالق الحب و النوى): Meaning the splitter of the grain and the pit. This is mentioned once for God in the Holy Qur'an:

"Indeed Allah is **the Splitter of the grain and the pit**. He brings forth the living from the dead and He brings forth the dead from the living. That is Allah! Then where do you stray?" (6:95)

10.4. Fāliq al-iṣbāh (فالق الاصباح): Meaning the splitter of the dawn. This is used as a divine quality once. The Qur'an says:

"Splitter of the dawn, He has made the night for rest, and the sun and the moon for calculation. That is the ordaining of the Almighty, All-knowing." (6:96)

10.5. **Khāliq** (خالق): Meaning creator. This is mentioned as a divine quality eight times. For example, the Qur'an says:

"That is Allah, your Lord, there is no god except Him, the **Creator** of all things; so worship Him. He watches over all things." (6:102)

10.6. **Khāliqūn** (خالقون): This is mentioned as a divine quality once in the Qura'n and is the plural form of *khāliq*, which means creator. The Qur'an says:

"Is it you who create it, or are We the **Creators**?" (56:59)

10.7. **Khallāq** (خلاق): Meaning the one who creates a lot. This is applied twice for God:

"Indeed your Lord is the **Creator**, the All-knowing." (15:86)

10.8. **Ahsan al-khāliqīn** (احسن الخالقين): Meaning the best of creators, this is mentioned twice in the Qur'an. One instance is:

"Then We created the drop of fluid as a clinging mass. Then We created the clinging mass as a fleshy tissue. Then We created the fleshy tissue as bones. Then We clothed the bones with flesh. Then We produced him as [yet] another creature. So blessed is Allah, the **Best** of creators!" (23:14)

10.9. **Muhyi al-mawtā** (محيى الموتى): Meaning reviver of the dead. This is applied twice to God. One example is in the following verse:

"So observe the effects of Allah's mercy: how He revives the earth after its death! Indeed He is the **Reviver** of the dead, and He has power over all things." (30:50)

10.10. **Mūsi'ūn (موسعون):** Meaning expander. This is used as a divine quality once:

"We have built the sky with might, and indeed it is We who are its **Expanders**." (51:47)

10.11. **Bāri (بارئ):** Meaning creator or maker. This is used for God three times. The verse below is one example:

"He is Allah, the Creator, **the Maker**, the Former. To Him belong the Best Names. Whatever there is in the heavens glorifies Him and [whatever there is in] the earth, and He is the Almighty, the Wise." (59:24)

10.12. **Muṣawwir (مصور):** Meaning the giver of form or shape. This is mentioned once in the Qur'an in the above verse, (59:24). Again, although the idea that God gives form to human beings is mentioned in several verses through the use of present tense or past tense verbs, here we are concerned only with the names and qualities directly attributed to God.

11. Truthfulness

11.1. **Haqq (حق):** Meaning truth, true or reality. This has been used 11 times in the Qur'an for God. For example, the Qur'an says:

"So exalted is Allah, the **True** Sovereign, There is no god except Him, the Lord of the Noble Throne." (23:116)

and

"That is because God is the **Truth**, and what they invoke besides Him is nullity, and because God is the All-exalted, the All-great." (22:62)

**11.2. Aşdaq-u hadithan (اصدق حديثًا): Meaning more truthful in speech. This is mentioned once:

"Allah - there is no god except Him - will surely gather you on the Day of Resurrection, in which there is no doubt; and who is **more truthful in speech** than Allah?" (4:87)

**11.3. Aşdaq-u qil-an (اصدق قيلا): Meaning more truthful in speech. This is mentioned once:

"But those who have faith and do righteous deeds, We will admit them into gardens with streams running in them, to remain in them forever a true promise of Allah, and who is **more truthful in speech** than Allah?" (4:122)

11.4. Sādiqūn (صادقون): This is the plural form for **şādiq and means truthful. This is used once in the Qur'an, in the following verse:

"To the Jews We forbade every animal having an undivided hoof, and of oxen and sheep We forbade them their fat, except what is borne by their backs or the entrails or what is attached to the bones. We requited them with that for their rebelliousness, and We are surely **Truthful**." (6:146)

12. Nearness: At the same time as speaking of God as a transcendent and exalted reality, the Qur'an also places great emphasis on the fact that God is very close to us. God is even closer to us than our jugular vein. We should always feel His presence. In the following passages, we refer to some of the qualities of God related to this aspect of His nearness.

12.1. Qarīb (قريب): Meaning close or near. This is used for God three times. For example, the Qur'an says:

> "When My servants ask you about Me, [tell them that] I am indeed **Near**. I answer the supplicant's call when he calls Me. So let them respond to Me, and let them have faith in Me, so that they may fare rightly." (2:186)

12.2. Shahīd (شهيد): This means witness or present. It is also sometimes used to be synonymous with martyr, because martyrs are thought to be living and present. There are 19 cases, in which the Qur'an emphasises that God is present and witnesses every thing. For example, the Qur'an says:

> "...to whom belongs the kingdom of the heavens and the earth, and Allah is **Witness** to all things." (85:9)

12.3. Shuhūd (شهود): This is the plural form of *shahid* and means witnesses. This is used for God once in the Holy Qur'an:

> "You do not engage in any work, neither do you recite any part of the Qur'an, nor do you perform any deed but We are **Witnesses** over you when you are engaged therein. Not an atom's weight escapes your Lord in the earth or in the sky, nor [is there] anything smaller than that nor bigger, but it is in a manifest Book." (10:61)

12.4. Raqīb (رقيب): This means watchful and is used three times in the Qur'an to refer to God. For example, the Qur'an says:

> "O mankind! Be wary of your Lord who created you from a single soul, and created its mate form it, and, from the two of them, scattered numerous men and women. Be wary of Allah, in whose Name you adjure one another, and the wombs. Indeed Allah is **Watchful** over you." (4:1)

12.5. Aqrab (أقرب): This means nearer and is attributed twice to God:

> "Certainly We have created man and We know to what his soul tempts him, and We are **Nearer** to him than his jugular vein." (50:16)

and

> "We are **Nearer** to him than you are, though you do not perceive." (56:85)

12.6. Zāhir (ظاهر): Literally meaning manifest or apparent, this has been used for God once:

> "He is the First and the Last, the **Manifest** and the Hidden, and He has knowledge of all things." (57:3)

12.7. Bāṭin (باطن): Literally meaning hidden or internal, this has been used for God in verse 57:3, above. It shows that God is present everywhere: in the manifest world and in the hidden world. He is manifest, but not so much so that we could fully grasp Him. He is hidden, but not so much so that He would be absent or remain unknown to us.

12.8. God is not ghā'ib (غائب): This means that God is never absent. In addition to those verses that affirm directly the fact that God is present and witnesses everything, in the following verse the Qur'an denies the absence of God. In this particular verse the plural form, (ghā'ibin) is used:

> "Then We will surely recount to them with knowledge, for We had not been **absent**." (7:7)

13. Life & eternity

13.1. Qayyūm (قيّوم): In Arabic, this term is used for something that is self-subsistent and supports other beings. This is mentioned as a divine quality three times. One example is:

"God, there is no god except Him, is the Living One, **the Sustainer**." (3:2)

13.2. Hayy (حى): Meaning the living. This is mentioned five times in the Qur'an as a quality of God. For example, the Qur'an says:

"He is **the Living** One, there is no god except Him. So supplicate Him, putting exclusive faith in Him. All praise belongs to Allah, the Lord of the Worlds." (40:65)

13.3. Wārithūn (وارثون): This is the plural form of wārith and means inheritors. It means that God remains and lasts forever and is mentioned as a quality for God twice in the Qur'an, such as in the following verse:

"Indeed it is We who give life and bring death and We are the **Inheritors**." (15:23)

13.4. Abqā (ابقى): Meaning more endurable or more lasting. This is attributed to God once and that is in the following verse:

"We have indeed believed in our Lord that He may forgive us our iniquities and the magic you compelled us to perform. Allah is **Better** and **More lasting**." (20:73)

13.5. Awwal (اول): Meaning the first. This is mentioned once in the Qur'an as a divine quality. It implies that God is eternal and nothing preceded Him in existence. The Qur'an says:

"He is **the First** and the Last, the Manifest and the Hidden, and He has knowledge of all things." (57:3)

13.6. **Ākhar** (آخر)**:** Meaning the last. This is mentioned as a divine quality once. It implies that God is everlasting. The Qur'an says:

"He is the First and the **Last**, the Manifest and the Hidden, and He has knowledge of all things." (57:3)

14. Justice

14.1. **Sarī' al-hisāb** (سريع الحساب)**:** Meaning swift to reckon. This has been applied to God eight times in the Qur'an. One of the verses is quoted here:

"Today every soul shall be requited for what it has earned. There will be no injustice today. Indeed Allah is **Swift at reckoning**." (40:17)

14.2. **Sarī' al-'iqāb** (سريع العقاب)**:** Meaning swift in punishment. This is mentioned as a divine quality twice. One of these verses is:

"It is He who has made you successors on the earth, and raised some of you in rank above others so that He may test you in respect to what He has given you. Indeed your Lord is **Swift in punishment**, and indeed He is All-forgiving, All-merciful." (6:165)

14.3. **Jāmi'** (جامع)**:** Meaning the gatherer. This is used as a quality for God twice, such as in the following verse:

"Our Lord! You are the **Gatherer** of mankind on a day in which there is no doubt. Indeed Allah does not break His promise." (3:9)

14.4. **Qā'im-an bi al-qist** (قائما بالقسط)**:** Meaning maintainer of justice. This has been attributed to God once, in the following verse:

"Allah bears witness that there is no god except Him and [so do] the angels and those who possess knowledge **Maintainer of justice**, there is no god but Him, the Almighty, the All-wise." (3:18)

14.5. Hasīb (حسيب): Meaning the reckoner. This is applied to God three times, since God takes account of all things. For example, the Qur'an says:

"When you are greeted with a salute, greet with a better one than it, or return it; indeed Allah is **Reckoner** of all things." (4:86)

14.6. Asra' al-hāsibīn (اسرع الحاسبين): Meaning the swiftest of the reckoners. This is once mentioned in the Qur'an as a divine quality:

"Then they are returned to Allah, their real master. Look! All judgement belongs to Him, and He is **the Swiftest of reckoners**." (6:62)

14.7. Hāsibīn (حاسبين): This is the plural form of *hasib* and means reckoners. It is mentioned once in the Qur'an for God:

"We shall set up the scales of justice on the Day of Resurrection, and no soul will be wronged in the least. Even if it be the weight of a mustard seed We shall produce it and We suffice as **Reckoners**." (21:47)

14.8. Khayr al-hākimīn (خيرالحاكمين): Meaning the best of judges. It is mentioned as a divine quality three times in the Qur'an. One of these is below:

"And follow that which is revealed to you, and be patient until Allah issues [His] judgement, and He is the **Best of judges**." (10:109)

14.9. **Ahkam al-hākimīn** (احكم الحـاكمين): Meaning the most just, the fairest of judges or the most capable of judges. It is mentioned as a divine quality twice. For example, the Qur'an says:

"Is not Allah **the Fairest of all judges?**" (95:8)

14.10. **'Aduww-un li al-kāfirīn** (عدو للكـافرين): Meaning an enemy of those who reject faith. This has been attributed once to God in the Qur'an in response to those who show enmity to God, His angels or His apostles:

"[Say] 'Whoever is an enemy of Allah, His angels and His apostles, and Gabriel and Michael, [let him know that] Allah is indeed **the Enemy of those who reject faith.**'" (2:98)

14.11. **Shadīd al-'iqāb** (شـديد العقـاب): Meaning severe in punishment. This is attributed to God 14 times. For example, the Qur'an says:

"Know that Allah is **Severe in punishment**, and that Allah is all-forgiving, all-merciful." (5:98)

14.12. **Shadīd al-'adhāb** (شـديد العذاب): This is similar to the previous quality and is mentioned once:

"Among the people are those who take others (for worship) besides Allah, loving them as if loving Allah but the faithful have a more ardent love for Allah though the wrongdoers will see, when they sight the punishment, that power, altogether, belongs to Allah, and that Allah is **Severe in punishment**." (2:165)

14.13. **Dhū intiqām** (ذوانتقـام): Meaning avenger. This is used for God four times in the Qur'an:

"...and whomever Allah guides, there is no one who can lead him astray. Is not God an Almighty **Avenger**?" (39:37)

14.14. **Ashadd-u tankīl-an** (اشد تنكيلا): Meaning severest in punishment. This is mentioned as a divine quality once:

"So fight in the way of Allah: you are responsible only for yourself, but urge on the faithful [to fight]. Maybe Allah will curb the might of the faithless, for Allah is Greatest in might and **Severest in punishment**." (4:84)

14.15. **Ahaqq-u an takhshawh-u** (احق ان تخشوه): This quality occurs twice in the Qur'an and means that God is worthier of fear. The idea is that the faithful should not be worried about what people may think about them or how they might act with them if they are doing something right. If they are doing something wrong and displeasing God, however, then it is a different matter.

"Will you not make war on a people who broke their pledges and resolved to expel the Apostle, and opened [hostilities] against you initially? Do you fear them? But Allah is **Worthier of being feared by you**, should you be faithful." (9:13)

14.16. **Ahaqq-u an yurdūh-u** (احق ان يرضوه): This has occurred once in the Qur'an and means that God is worthy of being pleased. It is used in the verse below:

"They swear to you by Allah, to please you; but Allah and His Apostle are **worthier that they should please Him**, should they be faithful." (9:62)

14.17. **Ahaqq-u an yuttaba'** (احق ان يتبع): This has occurred once in the Qur'an and means that He is the most worthy of being followed:

"Say, 'Is there anyone among your partners who may guide to the truth?' Say, 'Allah guides to the truth. Is he who guides to the truth **worthier to be followed**, or he who guides not unless he is [himself] guided? What is the matter with you? How do you judge?'" (10:35)

14.18. **Mundhirīn** (منذرين): This is the plural form of *mundhir* which means the one who gives warning. This is used for God once:

"Indeed We sent it down on a blessed night, and indeed We have been **Warning** [mankind]." (44:3)

14.19. **Muntaqimūn** (منتقمون): This is a plural form of *muntaqim*, which means avenger. There are three cases in the Qur'an where this has been attributed to God. One of them is the following verse:

"Who is a greater wrongdoer than him who is reminded of his Lord's signs, whereat he disregards them? Indeed We shall **take vengeance** upon the guilty." (32:22)

14.20. **Dhū 'iqāb-in 'alīm** (ذوعقاب اليم): Meaning the owner of painful punishment. This is used once in the Qur'an:

"Nothing is said to you except what has already been said [earlier] to the apostles before you. Indeed your Lord is Forgiving and **One who owns a painful retribution**." (41:43)

14.21. **Barī** (برئ من المشركين): This phrase is used once in the Qur'an and means that God is free from any obligation to the polytheists. This is mentioned at the beginning of the Chapter Nine:

"[This is] an announcement from Allah and His Apostle to all the people on the day of the greater Hajj that Allah and His Apostle **are free from obligation to the polytheists**. If you repent that is better for you; but if you turn your backs [on Allah], know that you cannot thwart Allah, and inform the faithless of a painful punishment." (9:3)

14.22. **Ahl al-taqwā (اهل التقوى):** Meaning the one who deserves that you should be wary of him. This is mentioned for God once:

"And they will not remember unless Allah wishes. He is **Worthy of [your] being wary [of Him]** and He is Worthy to forgive." (74:56)

14.23. God is not **zallām (ظلام):** This means that God is not in the least bit unjust (to the servants). This is emphasised in five verses, such as the following one:

"That is because of what your hands have sent ahead, and because Allah is not **in the least bit unjust to the servants.**" (8:51)

14.24. God is not **muhlik al-qurā bi zulm-in (مهلک القرى بظلم):** This literally means that God is not an unjust destroyer of the towns. The idea is that God never punishes people without warning them or more than what they deserve. This point is mentioned once in the Qur'an:

"This is because your Lord would **never destroy the towns unjustly** while their people were unaware." (6:131)

14.25. God is not **zālim (ظالم):** This means that God is not unjust. In addition to those verses that directly affirm the fact that God is the maintainer of justice or the most just of the judges, in the following verse the Qur'an denies the injustice of God. In this particular verse a plural form (ẓālimin) is used:

"...for the sake of admonition, and We **were not unjust**." (26:209)

15. Activeness: The Qur'an criticizes those who think that after creating the world, God has nothing to do with the world and its affairs. Indeed, creation is an ongoing process, which has never stopped. In what follows, we will refer to those attributes of God that indicate His active role in the world in general, and in human life in particular.

15.1. Waliyy (ولی): This has different meanings. However, the main meaning especially when it is used for God or for the people who are mentioned along with God, is the guardian, the custodian or the one who is in charge. This has been used in the Qur'an 12 times for God. For example, the Qur'an says:

> "Have they taken guardians besides Him? [Say,] 'It is Allah who is the **Guardian**, and He revives the dead, and He has power over all things.'" (42:9)

and

> "Your **guardian** is only God, His Apostle, and the faithful who maintain the prayer and give the zakat while bowing down." (5:55)[2]

15.2. Awlā (اولی): Meaning the one who has more authority or right for (doing) something than others. This is mentioned once in the Qur'an for God:

> "O you who have faith! Be maintainers of justice and witnesses for the sake of Allah, even if it should be against yourselves or [your] parents and near relatives, and whether it be [someone] rich or poor, for Allah is a **Better protector of** them [or has a greater right over them]. So do not follow [your] desires, lest you should be unfair, and if you distort

51

[the testimony] or disregard [it], Allah is indeed well aware of what you do." (4:135)

15.3. Mawlā (مولى): Again this has different meanings. However, the main meaning, especially when it is used for God, is master or guardian. This has been used in the Qur'an 12 times for God. For example, the Qur'an says:

"And if they turn away, then know that Allah is your **Master**: an excellent Master and an excellent Helper!" (6:40)

15.4. Khayr al-nāṣirīn (خيرالناصرين): Meaning best of helpers. This is used as a divine quality once in the Qur'an, in the following verse:

"Rather Allah is your Master, and He is **the Best of helpers**." (3:150)

15.5. Wakīl (وكيل): Meaning protector or guardian. This is mentioned as a divine quality 13 times in the Qur'an. One of these cases is:

"And put your trust in Allah; Allah suffices as **Protector**." (33:3)

15.6. Naṣīr (نصير): Meaning helper. This is used as divine quality 4 times in the Qur'an. One example is:

"But Allah knows your enemies better, and Allah suffices as guardian, and Allah suffices as **Helper**." (4:45)[3]

15.7. Khayr al-fātihīn (خير الفاتحين): Literally meaning the best of those who open or decide or judge. This is mentioned once in the Qur'an in the following verse:

"We would be fabricating a lie against Allah should we revert to your creed after Allah had delivered us from it. It does not behove us to return to it, unless Allah, our Lord should wish so. Our Lord embraces all things in [His] knowledge. In Allah we have put our trust. Our Lord! Decide between us and our people, and You are **the Best of deciders!**" (7:89)

In this verse, the believers ask God to decide or judge between them and those who reject faith. This may refer to the final judgement on the Day of Judgement. However, it is likely that it refers to a judgement or decision to be made by God in this world, to support and bring victory to the party of truth. Accordingly, this verse shows the active role that God plays in supporting the people of truth and good will.

15.8. **Mūhin-u kayd al-kāfirīn** (موهن كيد الكافرين): Meaning One who makes the plans of the faithless weak or feeble. This is mentioned as a divine quality once in the Qur'an:

"Such is the case, and [know] that Allah is the **One who makes weak the stratagems of the faithless**." (8:18)

15.9. **Khayr al-mākirīn** (خير الماكرين): Meaning the best of planners. This is used as a divine quality twice in the Qur'an, like in the following example:

"Then they [planned and] plotted, and Allah also planned, and Allah is the **Best of planners**." (3:54)

15.10. **Khādi'** (خادع): Literally meaning deceiver, this term is used once in the Qur'an for God and suggests that those who think they can deceive God only deceive themselves. They can never defeat God. The Qur'an says:

"The hypocrites indeed seek to deceive Allah, but it is He who **outwits** them. When they stand up for prayer, they stand up lazily, showing off to the people and not remembering Allah except a little." (4:142)

15.11. **Mukhzi al-kāfirīn** (مخزى الكافرين): In the following verse, God is introduced as the one who brings shame to the faithless and disgraces them:

"Travel [unmolested] in the land for four months, but know that you cannot thwart Allah, and that Allah shall **disgrace the faithless**." (9:2)

15.12. **Asra'-u makran** (اسرع مكرا): In the following verse, God is introduced as the one who is faster and swifter at planning than those who plot against the divine signs:

"When We let people taste [Our] mercy after distress that has befallen them, behold, they scheme against Our signs! Say, 'Allah is **Swifter at planning.**' Indeed Our messengers write down what you scheme." (10:21)

15.13. **Fa'āl-un limā yurīd** (فعال لما يريد): Meaning the great doer of what He wills. This is mentioned as a divine quality twice. For example, the Qur'an says:

"The Great doer of what He wills." (85:16)

15.14. **Musta'ān** (مستعان): Meaning the one whose help is sought. This is mentioned twice in the Qur'an. One of these is:

"He said, 'My Lord! Judge with truth.' 'Our Lord is the All-compassionate, **Whose help is sought** against what you ascribe.'" (21:112)

15.15. **Hādī** (هادى): Meaning guide. This is used as a divine quality twice in the Qur'an. For example:

"That is how for every prophet We assigned an enemy from among the guilty, and your Lord suffices as a **Guide and a Helper**." (25:31)

15.16. **Kāfi-n 'abdah-u (كاف عبده):** Meaning sufficient for his servant. This is mentioned as a divine quality once in the Holy Qur'an:

"Is not God **sufficient for His servant**? They would frighten you of others than Him. Yet whomever Allah leads astray, has no guide." (36:36)

15.17. **Fattāh (فتاح):** Meaning the greatest decider or judge. This is used as divine quality once in the Qur'an:

"Say, 'Our Lord will bring us together, then He will judge between us with truth, and He is the **Greatest decider**, the All-knowing.'" (34:26)

15.18. **Mu'min (مؤمن):** Meaning the securer. This is mentioned as a divine quality in the following verse:

"He is Allah there is no god except Him, the Sovereign, the All-holy, the All-benign, the **Securer**, the All-conserver, the Almighty, the All-compeller, the All-magnanimous. Clear is Allah of any partners that they may ascribe [to Him]!" (59:23)

15.19. **Bāligh-u amrih (بالغ امره):** Meaning the one who carries through his command or accomplishes his purpose. This is used once in the Qur'an for God. It means that God has full command of His affairs and whatever He decides certainly happens. The Qur'an says:

"...and provide for him from whence he does not reckon. And whoever puts his trust in Allah, He will suffice him. Indeed Allah **carries through His**

command. Certainly Allah has set a measure for everything." (65:3)

15.20. **Khayr al-rāziqīn** (خير الرازقين): Meaning the best of providers. This is used as a divine quality five times in the Qur'an. Two of these is in the following examples:

"Those who migrate in the way of Allah and then are slain, or die, Allah will surely provide them with a good provision. Allah is indeed **the Best of providers**." (22:58)

and

"Say, 'Indeed my Lord expands the provision for whomever of His servants that He wishes and tightens it, and He will repay whatever you may spend, and He is **the Best of providers**.'" (34:39)

15.21. **Razzāq** (رزاق): Meaning the provider. This is used as divine quality once:

"Indeed it is Allah who is the **Provider**, the Powerful, the Strong." (51:58)

15.22. **Zāri'ūn** (زارعون): This is attributed to God once in the Qur'an and is the plural form of *zāri'* which means **the one who makes things grow**. The Qur'an says:

"Is it you who make it grow, or are We the **ones who make it grow**?" (56:64)

15.23. **Munzilūn** (منزلون): This is the plural form of *munzil*, which literally means the one who sends down. This is mentioned twice in the Qur'an:

"Is it you who bring it down from the rain cloud, or are We the ones **who bring [it] down**?" (56:69)

and

"We are indeed **going to bring down** upon the people of this town a punishment from the sky because of the transgressions they used to commit." (29:34)

15.24. **Khayr al-munzilin** (خير المنزلين)**:** Meaning the best to bring ashore or the best to enable to disembark, this is mentioned as a divine quality once:

"And say, 'My Lord! Land me with a blessed landing, for You are the **Best of those who bring ashore**.'" (23:29)

15.25. **Munshi'ūn** (منشئون)**:** This is the plural form of *munshi'* which means producer. This is mentioned once in the Qur'an:

"Was it you who produced its tree, or were We the **Producers**?" (56:72)

Chart one: Divine names & attributes in the Qur'an

[other than Allâh (God), ilâh (god) & rabb (lord)]

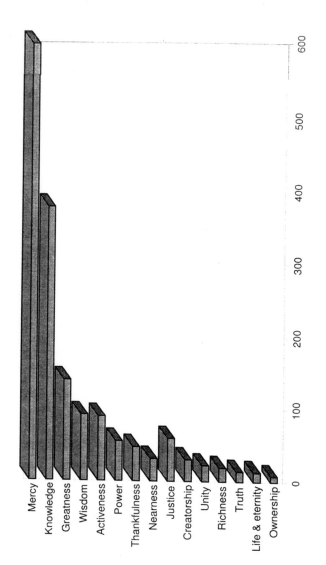

Endnotes

1. In verse 53:5, we read that the Prophet Mohammad was taught by **one of great powers** (شديد القوى). Some commentators of the Qur'an believe that this refers to God. For example, see *Tafsir-e Nemūneh*, Vol 22, pp. 487-490. There are others who believe that this refers to the Archangel Gabriel. For example, see *Majma' al-Bayān*, Vol. 9, p. 261.

2. In addition to those 12 cases, in which God is introduced as *waliyy*, there are 11 cases, in which the Qur'an emphasises that there is no waliyy who can replace God. There is also a case, in which the Qur'an denies the existence of any other wāli (والى; protector) besides God who could protect those who He wishes to visit with ill. See verse 13:11.

3. In addition to those 4 cases, in which God is introduced as *naṣir*, there are 7 cases, in which the Qur'an emphasises that there is no naṣir who can replace God.

God in Islamic Traditions: A Glance at *Al-Tahwid* by Shaykh al-Saduq

Dr Karim Aghili

After Kulayni, the second greatest Shi'te scholar of hadith was Abu Ja'far Muhammad b. Ali b. Husayn b. Musa b. Babawayh Qummi, commonly known as Shaykh al-Saduq. His exact date of birth is not known, but what we learn from his own book *Ikmāl al-Din* and Shaykh al-Tusi's *al-Ghaybah* and al-Najashi's *al-Fihrist* is that it is likely that he was born during the early years of the *safarah* (deputyship) of the third deputy (*nā'ib*) of the present Imam (*circa* 305/917-18) in the city of Qum.

Besides collecting and editing the books of hadith, al-Saduq trained a large number of pupils, who carried on preserving, collecting and narrating the traditions of the Shi'ite Imams throughout the Islamic world. He occupied a central place in the circle of the Shi'ite scholars and had a large number of followers.

Most of the researchers believe that al-Saduq wrote and compiled about three hundred books. The titles of two hundred and nineteen of these are given in the introduction of *Man la Yahduruhu al-Faqih* (For him not in the Presence of a Jurisprudent), which is the most important of all the extant works of al-Shaykh al-Saduq and one of the most famous and authoritative collections of Shi'ite hadiths. It is regarded as the second most important hadith collection after al-Kulayni's *Al-Kafi fi 'Ilm al-Din* (the Sufficient in the Knowledge of Religion).

What follows is a translation of a number of traditions (hadiths) selected from *Al-Tawhid* (the Unity of God), another very important work of Shaykh al-Saduq. It is taken from the edition edited by Sayyid Hashim Tehrani.

Al-Tawhid contains the most profound and delicate hadiths dealing with the issues pertaining to God, especially to the Unity of God from the perspective of the Shi'ite school of thought. The compiler has commented on some of the hadiths (traditions) contained in the book in the light of the Qur'an and the traditions of the Shi'ite Imams. Some Shi'ite scholars have written commentaries on this book and several of these have also been referred to by the editor in his introduction to the book.

Al-Tawhid contains 583 hadiths arranged in 67 chapters. In some manuscripts or editions, there are 66 chapters. This is due to either chapter 43 or chapter 49 being combined with its previous one. Every chapter deals with a specific issue, which is related to Divine Essence, Attributes or Acts.

Titles of the Chapters of al-Tawhid

1. Reward for the for the Monotheists and the Gnostics

2. Divine Unity and Negation of Anthropomorphism

3. The Meanings of the One, Divine Unity and the Monotheist

4. Commentary on "Say: He is Allah, the One. Allah is the All-everlasting. He neither begets nor was He begotten, nor has he any equal" (112).

5. The Meanings of Divine Unity and Justice

6. That He, the Majestic and Exalted, is not corporeal nor does He have a form.

7. That He, the Blessed and Exalted, is a Thing (*shay'*)

8. What has been said on the Vision [of God]

9. Divine Omnipotence

10. Divine Omniscience

11. Divine Essence, Attributes and Actions

12. Commentary on the saying of God, the Exalted and Majestic: "Everything is perishable save His Face." (28: 88)

13. Commentary on the saying of God, the Exalted and Majestic: "O Iblis! What keeps you from prostrating before that which I have created with My [own] two hands?" (38:75)

14. Commentary on the saying of God, the Exalted and Majestic: "That day when the catastrophe occurs, and they are summoned to prostrate themselves, and they will not be able [to do it]." (68:42)

15. Commentary on the saying of God, the Exalted and Majestic: "God is the Light of the heavens and the earth...."(24:35)

16. Commentary on the saying of God, the Exalted and Majestic: "They have forgotten God, so God has forgotten them." (9:67)

17. Commentary on the saying of God, the Exalted and Majestic: "...yet the entire earth will be in His fist on the Day of Resurrection, and the heavens, scrolled, in His right hand." (39:67)

18. Commentary on the saying of God, the Exalted and Majestic: "No Indeed! They will be alienated from their Lord on that day." (83:15)

19. Commentary on the saying of God, the Exalted and Majestic: "... and your Lord and the angels arrive in ranks." (89:22)

20. Commentary on the saying of God, the Exalted and Majestic: "Do they await anything but that God ['s command] should come to them in the shades of the clouds, with the angels." (2:210)

21. Commentary on the sayings of God, the Exalted and Majestic: "God shall put them to ridicule" (9:79); "Then they plotted [against Jesus] and God also devised, and God is the Best of

devisers" (3:54); "The hypocrites indeed seek to deceive God, but it is He who outwits them" (4:142).

22. The Meaning of the Vicinity of God, the Exalted and Majestic

23. The Meaning of *al-hujzah* [originally, the place where the trousers or kilt is fastened; it is also used in the sense of trousers and kilts themselves].

24. The Meanings of the eye, the ear, and the tongue.

25. The Meaning of the Saying of God, the Exalted and Majestic: "The Jews say, 'God's hand is tied up.' Tied be their hands, and cursed be they for what they say! Rather, His hands are wide open." (5:64)

26. The Meanings of Divine Approval (*ridā*) and Wrath (*sakhat*)

27. The Meaning of the Saying of God, the Exalted and Majestic: "..and breathed into him of My spirit." (15:29)

28. Negation of Space, Time, Rest, Motion, Descent, Ascent and Change of location of God, the Exalted and Majestic.

29. The Names of God and the Difference between their Meanings and Those of the Creatures

30. The Nature of the Qur'an

31. The Meaning of 'In the Name of God, All-merciful, Most-merciful'

321. Commentary on the Letters of the Alphabet (*hurūf al-muʻjam*)

33. Commentary on the Letters of Calculation (*hurūf al-jumal*)

34. The Meanings of the Words of the Call to Prayers and the Declaration of Standing for Prayer

35. Commentary on Right Guidance, Error, Success, and Being Forsaken by God

36. Refutation of Dualism and Atheism

37. Refutation of Those "who say, 'God is the third [person] of a trinity', while there is no except the One God." (5:73)

38. Mentioning the Tremendousness of God, the Blessed and Majestic

39. The Gentleness of God, the Blessed and Exalted

40. The minimum necessary amount of the knowledge of Divine Unity

41. Surely He, the Exalted and the Majestic, cannot not be known except through Himself

42. Proof of the Temporality of the World

43. The Tradition of Dhi'lib

44. The Tradition of al-Sabkhat, the Jew

45. The Meaning of Glory be to God!

46. The Meaning of God is Greater.

47. The Meanings of the First and the Last

48. The Meaning of the Saying of God, "The All-merciful, settled on the Throne." (20:5)

49. The Meaning of the Saying of God, "and His Throne was [then] upon the water." (11:7)

50. The Throne and its Qualities

51. The Throne was the fourth thing to be created

52. His seat embraces the heavens and the earth (2:255).

53. God originated creation upon [innate knowledge of] His Oneness

54. Change of Destiny (*badā'*)

55. Divine Intention and Will

56. The Ability [of human beings]

57. Putting to the Test and Trial

58. Felicity and Misery

59. Refutation of Compulsion and Complete Freedom

60. Divine Decree (*qaḏā*) and Measure (*qadar*), Sedition, Provisions, Prices, and the Appointed Times

61. Children and the Justice shown to them by God, the Exalted and Majestic, towards them

62. God, the Exalted, does not deal with His servants except based on that which is in their best interest

63. Command, Prohibition, Promise and Threat

64. Information, Explanation, Proof and Guidance

65. Imam Riḏā's meeting, peace be upon him, with the people of the different religions and the people of different beliefs, such as Jathiliq (Catholicos), Ra's al-Jālūt (Exilarch, lit. 'Head of the Exile'), the chiefs of the Sabaeans, Chief Hirbud, and what 'Imrān al-T'ābi'i said on Divine Unity in the presence of al-Ma'mun

66. Imam Riḍā's Meeting, peace be upon him, with Sulayman al-Marwazi, the theologian of Khurasan on Divine Unity in the presence of al-Ma'mun

67. Prohibiting Disputing and Arguing about God, the Exalted and Majestic

The Unity of God is the foundational principle of all the revealed religions. Hence, a follower of the Islamic religion must first accept the testimony of faith: 'There is no god but God'. It is this profession of God's Unity, which is Islam's first pillar and all else depends upon and is derived from it. In what follows, I will refer to three exemplar hadiths on divine attributes, narrated by Shaykh al-Saduq in *Al-Tawhid*. The following hadiths are all from the Chapter on "Divine Unity and Negation of Anthropomorphism".

1. Hadith number 27: Muhammad b. Muhammad b. 'Isam al Kulaini, may God have mercy upon him, narrated to us from Muhammad b. Ya'qub al-Kulaini that: Muhammad b. 'Ali b. 'Ātikah from al-Hasan b. Naār al-Fihri from 'Amr al-Awzā'i from 'Amr b. Shimr from Jabir b. Yazid al-Ju'fi from Abi Ja`far Muhammad b. `Ali al-Baqir from his father from his grandfather, peace be upon them, who said: The commander of the faithful said in a sermon that he delivered seven days after the death of the Prophet, when he had finished collecting the holy Qur'an:

> "All praise belongs to God, Who made it impossible for imaginations to comprehend His existence, and veiled their intellects from being able to imagine His essence, because it is impossible for His essence to have a like or form. His essence does not vary nor is it divided by numerical division in its [attributes of] perfection.

> "He is separated from things not in terms of distance, and within them not in terms of mixing, and knows [things] not by instruments [while others] cannot attain knowledge except through them. There is no

67

other knowledge than His between that which is known by Him and Him [so that He may need it to know things]. If it is said that 'He was', it should be interpreted as the pre-eternity of [His] existence. If 'still' is said of Him, it should be interpreted as the negation of non-existence [of His Essence].

"Glory be to Him, and high is He exalted above what those who worship other than Him say and who take a god other than Him.

"We praise Him with a praise that He accepted for His servants and with a praise that He made its acceptance obligatory upon them. I profess that there is no god but God, without any associate and profess that Muhammad is His servant and messenger. These two professions of faith elevate words and double [the weight of] deeds. The scale will become light when these two professions of faith are taken away from it, and it will be weighty if they are put in it. The attainment of Paradise, being saved from Hell, and crossing the path successfully are gained through these two professions of faith. You will enter Paradise by the two professions of faith and attain Divine mercy by prayer. Hence, invoke blessings on your Prophet and his Household frequently. "Indeed God and His angels bless the Prophet; O you who have faith! Invoke blessings on him and invoke Peace upon him in a worthy manner." (33:56)

"O people, surely there is no honour higher than Islam, no generosity more precious than mindfulness of God, no stronghold more protective than piety, no intercessor more beneficial than repentance, no treasure more beneficial than knowledge; no glory higher than forbearance, no noble descent more lasting than good manners, no fatigue more exhausting than anger, no beauty better than intelligence, no evil worse than falsehood, no guardian more protective than silence, no dress more beautiful than good health, and no absence closer than death.

"O people, whoever walks on the surface of the earth will eventually go beneath it. Day and night make haste to bring to an end life spans. Every possessor of the breath of life has provisions and every seed has an eater.

"You are the food of death. He who realizes the [vicissitudes of] time will not neglect readiness [for the hereafter]. Neither the wealth of the rich nor the poverty of the poor will save them from death. O people, he who fears His Lord will stop his wrongdoing. Whoever is not pious in his speech is more manifest in remoteness [from his Lord]. He who cannot distinguish good from evil is the same as an animal. How scanty are worldly misfortunes compared with the huge neediness of tomorrow. Your enmity is but due to your committing sins and acts of disobedience to God. Rest is very close to fatigue, and misery is very close to change. Any evil that is followed by Paradise is not a true evil, and any welfare that is followed by Hell is not a true welfare. Every comfort other than Paradise is valueless. Every misfortune other than Hell is good health."

2. Hadith number 26: Abu'l-'Abbas Muhammad b. Ibrahim b. Ishaq al-Ēāliqāni, may God be pleased with him, narrated to us this hadeeth, saying: "Abu Sa'id al-Hasan b. Ali al-'Adawi said: "al-Haitham b. Abd al-Allah al-Rummani narrated to us: 'Ali b. Musa al-Ridā narrated to me, from his father, Musa b. Ja'far from his father, Ja'far b. Muhammad on the authority of his father Muhammad b. 'Ali from his father 'Ali b. al-Husain from his

father al-Hasan b. 'Ali, peace be upon them, saying: 'The Commander of the Faithful (peace be upon him)addressed the people in the mosque at Kufa and said:

"All praise belongs to God, who does not exist because of anything and who did not bring that which exists into existence out of anything. He attests to His pre-eternity through the temporality (*hudūth*) of things, to His power through the impotence with which He has branded them, and to His everlastingness through the 'annihilation (*fanā'*) which He has forced upon them. No place is empty of Him so that He might be perceived through location, and nothing is like Him so that He might be described by quality, and He is not hidden from anything so that He might be known through comparison.

"He is distinct in terms of attributes from all that He has originated, impossible of perception because of the changing essences which He has created, and transcends all changing states because of grandeur and tremendousness. His delimitation is forbidden to penetrating and surpassing sagacity, His description to the piercing depths of thought and His representation to the penetrating and insightful probes.

"Because of His tremendousness, places do not encompass Him, because of His majesty measures cannot gauge Him, and because of His grandeur standards cannot judge Him. It is impossible for imaginations to fathom Him, understandings to comprehend Him or minds to imagine Him. High-aspiring powers of reason despair of contriving to comprehend Him, oceans of knowledge run dry without alluding to Him in depth, and the subtleties of disputants fall from loftiness to pettiness in describing His power.

70

"He is One not in terms of number; Everlasting, without duration; Standing, without supports, He is not of a kind that [other] kinds should be on a par with Him, nor an object that objects should be similar to Him, nor like things that attributes should apply to Him. Powers of reason go astray in the waves of the current of perceiving Him, imaginations are bewildered at encompassing the mention of His pre-eternity, understandings are incapable of becoming conscious of the description of His power, and minds are drowned in the depths of the heavens of His kingdom (*malakūt*).

"He possesses mastery over [giving] bounties, inaccessible through Grandeur, and Sovereign over all things. Time does not make Him old, nor does description encompass Him. The firmest of obstinacies in the limits of their constancy are humbled before Him, and the most unbreakable of the ropes in the extremity of their towering regions are submitted to Him.

"The totality of the different kinds [of creatures] attests to His Lordship, their impotence to His Power, their creation to His eternity, and their extinction to His permanence. So they possess no place of refuge from His grasp of them, no exit from His encompassing them, no way of veiling themselves from His enumeration of them and no way of avoiding His power over them. Sufficient is the perfection of His making them, (creatures) as a sign [of His creation], His compounding of their (natural) constitutions as a proof, the temporal origin of their natures as (a reason for His) eternity, and the creation's laws governing them as a lesson. No limit is attributed to Him, no similitude struck for Him and

71

nothing veiled from Him. Indeed He is far above the striking of similitude and above creaturely attributes.

"And I testify that there is no god but He and have faith in His lordship and oppose whoever denies Him; and I testify that Muhammad is His servant and messenger, who resides in the best lodging-place and passed from the noblest of loins and immaculate wombs, extracted in lineage from the noblest of mines and in origin from the most excellent of plantations. and (derived) from the most inaccessible of peaks and the most glorious roots, from the tree from which God fashioned His prophets and chose His trusted ones: [a tree] of excellent wood, harmonious stature, lofty branches, flourishing limbs, ripe fruit, noble interior. and was implanted in generosity and cultivated in a sacred precinct. There it put forth branches and fruit. became strong and unassailable, and then made him (the prophet Muhammad) tall and eminent, until God, the Mighty and Majestic, honoured him with the Faithful Spirit, the Illuminating Light, and the Manifest Book. He subjected to him Buraq and the angels greeted him. By means of him He terrified the devils, overthrew the idols and the gods (who were) worshipped apart from Him. His prophet's way (*sunnah*) is integrity, his conduct is justice and his decision is truth. He complied with that which his Lord commanded and proclaimed that with which he was charged with until he made plain his mission through the profession of Unity and made manifest among the creatures that there is no god but God alone and that He has no associate; until His Oneness became pure and His lordship unmixed. God made manifest his argument through the profession of His Unity and He raised his degree with submission. And God, the Mighty and Majestic, chose for His prophet what was with Him of repose, degree and means and God bless him and his pure household."

3. Hadith number 2: Muhammad b. al-Hasan b. Ahmad b. al-Walid, may God be pleased with him, narrated the following to us from Muhammad b. 'Amr al-Katib who narrated from Muhammad b. Abi Ziyad al-Qulzumi from Muhammad b. Abi Ziyad al-Juddi, the leader of the prayer in Jaddah, who said that Muhammad b. Yahya b. 'Umar b. 'Ali b. Abi Talib related to him: 'I heard Aba'l-Hasan b. al-Rida talking in this way about Divine Unity (*tawhid*) in the presence of al-Ma`mun. Ibn Abi Ziyad said: Ibn Abd al-Allah al-'Alawi, their master and the uncle of some of them, also related it to me from al-Qasim b. Ayyub al-'Alawi: When al-Ma'mun desired to appoint al-Rida [as his successor] he gathered together Banu Hashim and said to them, "Surely, I wish to appoint al-Ridā in this affair after me."

'Banu Hashim envied al-Ridā and said, "You [wish to] appoint an ignorant man who does not possess the insight to direct the caliphate? Send for him. He will come to us and you will see how his ignorance proves to be against him." So he sent for him and he came. Banu Hashim said to him, "O Abu'l-Hasan! Ascend the pulpit and raise for us a banner by which we may worship God. So he ascended the pulpit and sat for a long time, his head bowed in silence. Then he trembled a great trembling and stood up straight, praised and lauded God, and asked His blessing for His prophet and his household. Then he said:

> ' "The first act of worship of God is knowledge of Him, the root of knowledge of Him is to profess His Unity, and the correct way to profess the Unity of God is to negate attributes from Him. For the powers of reason testify that every attribute and everything having an attribute is created. Everything that has an attribute testifies that it has a Creator, which is neither an attribute nor possesses an attribute. Every attribute and everything that has an attribute testifies to a

connection between the attribute and that the thing to which it is attributed. Connection testifies to temporal origination, and temporal origination testifies that it does not accept pre-eternity, which refutes temporality.

"So it is not God whose Essence is known through comparison. It is not His Unity that is professed by someone who attempts to fathom Him. It is not His reality that is attained by someone who strikes a similitude for Him. It is not He who is confirmed by him who professes an end for Him. It is not He to who someone who points to Him turns to. It is not He who is meant by him who compares Him [to something]. It is not to Him that he who divides Him into parts humbles himself. And it is not He who is desired by him who conceives of Him in his imagination.

"Everything that can be known in itself is created. All that stands apart from Him is an effect. God is inferred from what He fashions, the knowledge of Him is made firm by the powers of reason, and the argument for Him is established by original human nature. God's creating of the creatures is a veil between Him and them. His separation from them is that He is disengaged from their localization. That He is their origin is proof for them that He has no origin, for whatever has an origin cannot originate others. That He has created them possessing the means needed for accomplishing things is proof that He has no means, for means are witness to the poverty of those who use them.

"So His names are an expression, His acts are [a means of] making [Him] understood, and His Essence is Reality, His innermost centre separates Him from creation, and His otherness limits what is other than

Him. Therefore, he who asks for Him to be described is ignorant of God! Transgressing against Him is he who seeks to encompass Him! He who imagines to have fathomed Him is mistaken!

"Whoever says 'how?' has compared Him [to something]. Whoever says 'why?' has professed for Him a cause. Whoever says 'when?' has determined Him in time. Whoever says 'in what?' has enclosed Him. Whoever says 'to what?' has professed for Him a limit. Whoever says 'until what?' has given Him an end. Whoever gives Him an end has associated an end with Him. 'Whosoever associates an end with Him has divided Him. Whoever divides Him has described Him. Whoever describes Him has deviated from the straight path concerning Him.

"God does not change with the changes undergone by creation, just as He does not become limited by delimiting that which is limited. He is One. Not according to the explanation offered by number; Outward, not according to the explanation of being immediate (to the senses); Manifest, not through the appearance of a vision [of Him]; Inward, not through separation; Apart, not through distance; Near, not through approach; Subtle, not through corporealization; Existent, not after non-existence; Active, not through coercion; Determining, not through the activity of thought; Directing not through movement; Desiring, not through resolution; Willing, not through directing attention; Grasping not through touch; Hearing, not through means; and Seeing, not through organs.

"Times do not accompany Him, places do not enclose Him, slumber does not seize Him, attributes do not delimit Him, and instruments are of no use to Him.

His being precedes time, His existence non-existence and His beginninglessness beginning.

"By His giving sense to the sense organs it is known that He has no sense organs. By His giving substance to substances it is known that He has no substance. By His creating opposition among things it is known that He has no opposite. By His causing affiliation among affairs it is known that He has no affiliate. He opposed darkness to light, obscurity to clarity, moisture to solidity, and heat to cold. He joins together those things that are hostile to one another and separates those that are near. They prove their Separator by their separation and their Joiner by their junction, that is [the meaning of] His words - He is the Mighty and Majestic – "And We created pairs of all things so that you [people] might take note." (51:49).

"So through them He separated 'before' and 'after' so that it might be known that He has no before and after. They testify with their temperaments that He who gave them temperaments has no temperament. They prove through their disparity that He who made them disparate has no disparity. They announce, through their being time-bound that He who subjected them to time is not subject to it Himself.

"He veiled some of them from others so that it might be known that there is no veil between Him and them other than them. His is the meaning of lordship when there was nothing over whom He was Lord, the reality of godhood when there was nothing for whom He was God, the meaning of Creator when there was nothing created and Knower when there was nothing knowable, the meaning and the import of hearing when there was nothing audible. It is not because He created that He deserves the meaning (of the term)

Creator and not because He brought the creatures into being that the meaning of nothing is derived.

"How [should it not be so]? For *mudh* (ever since) does not conceal Him, *qad* (already) does not bring Him near, *la'alla* (perhaps) does not veil Him, *matā* (when?) does not limit Him in time, *hin* (at the time of) does not contain Him, and *ma'a* (with) does not bring Him into association.

"Instruments (*adawāt*) limit only themselves and means (*ālah*) allude only unto their own like. Their activities are found only in things. *Mudh* withholds things from being eternal, *qad* shields them from without beginning, and *law lā* (if only) wards off perfection. Things become separate and prove (the existence of) their Separator. They become distinguished and prove their Distinguisher. Through them their Maker manifests Himself to the powers of reason. Through (these powers) He becomes veiled to sight, to them imaginations appeal for a decision, in them is substantiated (only) other than Him, from them is suspended the proof and through them He makes known to them the acknowledgement.

"Confirmation of God is made firm by the powers of reason, and faith in Him perfection is reached through acknowledgment. There is no religiosity except after knowledge, no knowledge except through sincerity and no sincerity along with comparison. There is no negation of comparison if there is affirmation of attributes.

"So nothing in creation is found in its Creator. All that is possible in it is impossible in its Maker. Movement and rest do not affect Him. How should that which He effects [in others] have effect upon Him, or 'that which He has originated recur for Him? Then His

Essence would be disparate, His innermost centre divided, His significance prevented from eternity. How would the Creator have a meaning different from the created?

"If something from behind limited Him, then something in front would limit Him. If perfection were seeking Him, imperfection would be upon Him. How should that which is impossible of temporality be worthy of pre-eternity? How should that which is not impossible of being produced produce things? Then there would have arisen in Him a sign of createdness and He would become a proof after having been the proven.

"There is no argument in absurd opinions, no answer when it [absurdity] is asked about, no glorification of Him in its meaning. There is no harm in distinguishing Him from creation unless it is that the Eternal is impossible of [accepting] duality, nor does the Pre-eternal have a beginning.

"There is no god but God, the All-high, the Tremendous. They have told lies who ascribe equals to God! They have gone into extreme error and incurred a manifest loss. And God bless Muhammad and his household, the pure.'"

The Qur'anic Proof for the Existence of God

Ayatollah Dr Sayyid Mohammad H. Beheshti
Translated from Persian by Dr. Karim Aghili

It is apparent from many verses in the Qur'an, some of which we will quote, that in the environment within which this divine book was revealed, the principle of the existence of God, the Creator of the Universe, was accepted by the majority of people, including the idolatrous Arabs.

> "And if you ask them: Who created the heavens and the earth and made the sun and the moon subservient, they will certainly say: God. Whence are they then turned away?" (29:61)

and

> "And if you ask them: Who is it that sends down water from the clouds, then gives life to the earth with it after its death, they will certainly say, Allah. Say: All praise is due to Allah. Nay, most of them do not understand." (29:63).

and

> "And if you [Prophet] ask them: Who created the heavens and the earth? they are sure to say: They were created by the Almighty, the All-knowing.' It is He who has smoothed out the earth for you and traced out routes on it for you to find your way, who sends water down from the sky in due measure –We resurrect dead land with it, and likewise you will be resurrected from the grave-who created every kind of thing, who gave you ships and animals to ride on." (43:9-12).

Also, in some other verses of the Qur'an, the idolatrous Arabs are quoted as explicitly acknowledging the existence of God, as in the following verse:

"And they serve besides Allah what can neither harm them nor profit them, and they say: These are our intercessors with Allah. Say: Do you (presume to) inform Allah of what He knows not in the heavens and the earth? Glory be to Him, and supremely exalted is He above what they set up (With Him)." (10:18).

It is clear from the above verses that the polytheists believed in the idols as intermediaries between them and God. This indicates their belief in the existence of God, the Creator.

Can there be any Doubt about God's Existence?

In the tenth verse of the Chapter named Abraham (Ibrähim) in the Qur'an, there is a sentence that reads,

"... is there any doubt about God Who is the Originator of the heavens and the earth?"

It has been repeatedly seen that some people have interpreted this verse in religious discussions as meaning that the Qur'an considers any doubt about God's existence baseless and that it considers the existence of God to be so self-evident for all those who reflect on the creation of the heavens and the earth that it needs no argument. However, some prominent Qur'anic commentators have disagreed with this interpretation. In order to shed light upon this issue, we would first like to quote verses 9 to 12 of this chapter in full:

"Has not the account reached you of those before you, of the people of Nuh and 'Ad and Thamud, and those after them? None knows them but Allah. Their apostles came to them with clear arguments, but they thrust their hands into their mouths and

80

said: 'Surely We deny that with which you are sent, and most surely we are in serious doubt as to that to which you invite us.'

"Their apostles said: 'Can there be any doubt about [the existence of] God, the Originator of the heavens and the earth? He invites you to forgive you your faults and to [give you] respite till an appointed term.' They said: 'You are nothing but mortals like us: you wish to turn us away from what our fathers used to worship; bring us therefore some clear authority.'

"Their apostles said to them: 'We are nothing but mortals like yourselves, but Allah bestows (His) favours on whom He pleases of His servants, and it is not for us that we should bring you an authority except by Allah's permission; and on Allah should the believers rely.

"And what reason have we that we should not rely on Allah? And He has indeed guided us in our ways; and certainly we would bear with patience you persecutions of us; and on Allah should the reliant rely.'" (14:9-12).

The people of Nuh, `Ad, Thamud, and others who followed them argued with the Prophets of God who had come to save them over the substance of the message delivered by them and explicitly stated that they did not believe in the substance of their call. Was the message of these prophets concerned with proving the existence of God or did the idol-worshipers among the people, as the Arab idol-worshippers during the lifetime of the Prophet of Islam, believe in the existence of the Creator of the universe and worship the idols as His visible manifestations who could fulfil their needs and act as intermediaries between them and their Creator?

In his Qur'anic commentary *Al-Mizan* (The Balance), Allamah Tabatabai, supports the second view and clearly states that the main issues between these people and their Prophets were the Oneness of God (*Tawhid*), prophecy (*nubuwwa*), and the resurrection (*ma`ad*), and not God's existence. From the words of Tabarsi and Sayyid Qutb in their respective books, *Majma' al-Bayān* and *Fi Ûilāl al-Qur'an*, and also from some of the other commentators, it can be concluded that they agreed with the latter view too. That is, the issues at stake were the Oneness of God, His unique dominion over the universe, the prophecy of these chosen men, divine reward and punishment in this world and the next and so on, but not the actual existence of God. Nevertheless, the exact wording of the Prophets is: 'Can there be any doubt about the existence of God Who is the Originator of the heavens and the earth?'

This expression in itself is concerned with doubt about the very existence of God, particularly since God's quality of being the Originator of the heavens and the earth is mentioned. Here, the word *Fāṭir* meaning originator has been used, because coming into existence, by *creatio ex nihilo* (creation out of nothing) is more consistent with arguing for the principle of the existence of the Creator than for His Oneness.

In *Al-Mizān*, Allamah Tabatabai considers this very expression as evidence for the soundness of his own view and says that if the phrase 'the Creator of the heavens and the earth' had been used, it would been appropriate for proving the existence of the Creator, but since the idol-worshippers did not deny the existence of the Creator of the universe, but denied the oneness of that Creator, the expression 'the Originator' had been used so that it might be congruous with the Oneness of God.[1]

However, in our view, the expression 'the Originator of the heavens and the earth' is even more appropriate than the phrase `the Creator of the heavens and the earth' for proving the existence of the Creator of the universe.

If it were true that all the Arab idol-worshippers during the lifetime of the Prophet did not deny the existence of God but only denied His unique governance of the universe and the fact that He alone is worthy of worship, the question arises as to whether this also holds true for the idol-worshippers of all the ages. If it does, we can rely on this fact to understand the verse relating to 'Ad, Thamud and other people of the past.

Furthermore, how can the origination of the heavens and the earth be a convincing proof for the Oneness of God, while it may not be a convincing proof for the principle of the existence of God?

Therefore, it should be accepted that this verse also pertains to the existence of God. However, the view that the Qur'an considers doubting the existence of God the same as doubting a self-evident principle, is not quite justified. The reason is that the expression 'the Originator of the heavens and the earth' mentioned in the verse above lays stress on the argument for the existence of God and not on the self-evidence of His existence or His existence being in no need of proving.

Furthermore, it is understood from some other verses in the Qur'an that in this Book which makes things clear, doubting the very existence of God has not been totally ignored either.

The chapter named *al-T'ūr* (the Mountain) is one of the chapters that was revealed in Mecca before the Prophet's move to Medina or *al-hijra* (the emigration). This chapter first brings up the doubt about the resurrection (*ma'ād*) in verses 1-28 and addresses those who do not believe in the Resurrection in detail. In verses 29-34, it deals with the doubt about the prophecy of the Prophet and refutes it. Then, it goes on to point out man's probable doubt about God as follows:

> "Or Were they created without there being anything, or are they creators?

"Or did they create the heavens and the earth? Nay, they have no certainty." (52: 35-6).

Also in the following verses, such questions as the following are raised: has man gained access to the treasures of God's mercy or does he himself have control over everything? Does he have access to the source of revelation?

Then in verse 43, the question of the existence of a god other than God, the Creator, is raised in the following way:

"Or have they a god other than Allah? Glory be to Allah from what they set up (with Him)."

In view of what has been said about the subject-matter of this chapter, it seems that in verses 35 and 36, it first raises the doubt about whether there is a creator for the creation of the universe and man or if they have all come into existence by themselves.

Then, in order to remove the doubt, [an approach similar to] the Socratic method[2] is used and, through some thought-provoking questions put to man, his innate reason is awakened in order for him to find the proper answers to the questions by thinking closely about them.

The questions are posed in the following order:

1. Can human beings have come into existence without a creator?

2. Can they have been their own creators?

3. If man were his creator, how should he account for the creation of the heavens and the earth that existed before man's creation? Can man have created them?

It seems that by posing such meaningful and thought-provoking questions, the Qur'an seeks to awaken the innate reason of man and elicit his answers so that he can say in answer to the first question:

'No, if human beings are creatures, they must certainly have a Creator.'

And in answer to the second question:

'And if they are creatures, they can never be their own creators. Not only human beings but all other creatures cannot be their own creators either, because an existent whose existence is derived from itself has always existed and will still exist and thus cannot be a 'creature' so that we can say that it is both a creature and a creator.'

And in answer to the third question by confessing:

'Although man possesses a creative power through which he creates such beautiful works of art as paintings and statues and makes missiles, cars, airplanes, and computers, he is fully aware of the fact that he has had nothing to do with the creation of the heavens and the earth. Therefore, is it not a funny sense of pride if he claims divinity by relying on his limited power and say: 'If there is a creator in the world, it is none other than man.''

Of course, in this regard, there are also other assumptions or hypotheses to which the Qur'an does seek to refer, but the point to be noted is that calling the existence of God into question is clearly evident from the foregoing verses.

The Story of the Prophet Abraham

Is this Story Related to God's Existence? In verses 74 to 79 of the Chapter named *An'ām (Cattle)*, Abraham is quoted as saying:

"(Remember) when Abraham said unto his father Azar, 'Takest thou idols for gods? Lo! I see thee and thy folk in error manifest.'

"Thus did We show Abraham the kingdom of the heavens and the earth that he might be of those possessing certainty.

"When the night grew dark upon him he beheld a star. He said, 'This is my Lord.' But when it set, he said, 'I love not things that set.'

"And when he saw the moon rising, he exclaimed, 'This is my Lord.' But when it set, he said, 'Unless my Lord guide me, I surely shall become one of the folks who are astray.'

"And when he saw the sun uprising, he cried, 'This is my Lord! This is greater!' And when it set, he exclaimed, 'O my people! Lo! I am free from all that ye associate (with him).'

"Lo! I have turned my face toward Him who created the heavens and the earth, as one by nature upright, and I am not of the idolaters.'" (6:74-79).

This story does not directly prove the existence of the Creator, but rather it pertains to the question of the Oneness of God, that is, the oneness of lordship, the governance of the world, and the Oneness of worship. However, at the same time the most noteworthy point in the story that is stressed by Abraham in his consideration of the creatures of this world and their being worthy or unworthy of divinity is that an existent [such as the sun], which is ephemeral and which sets, is a dependent existent. This in itself is a sign of an independent being, its creator and lord. Therefore, Godhead is due to the Creator who rules but not to a creature that is ruled.

Mulla Sadra considers this interpretation relevant to the argument for the existence of the Creation based on the laws of the natural sciences and says in *Al-Mabda' w'al-Ma'ād* (*The Origin and the Return*):

And the naturalists have adopted a specific path for the attainment of this end, and they explain it by saying, 'The motion of the heavenly bodies is an outward [observed] one which is neither by nature nor is it by constraint but rather they derive from the [heavenly] souls and from the desire for an inevitable end.[3]

'And as the end is not one of passion or anger, because it transcends them nor is it from the [other] bodies which lie below or above them nor from the souls connected to them as you will come to know the explanation of them all by means of argument.

Therefore, it has been specified that their end is a sacred one and is totally separated from matter [immaterial] and which possesses an infinite power and whose [powers of] putting into motion are not for the [attainment] of perfection. If its existence is necessary, the object of quest has been achieved, and if it is not necessary, it will lead to that whose existence is necessary and which refutes the vicious circle and infinite regress.

This is the path as adopted and relied on by the master of Peripatetic [Aristotle] in the two sections on the natural hearing of physics and on the principles of theology of his Book entitled the First Teaching. The path has been referred to in the Divine Book's narration of the story of Abraham, peace be upon him, our Prophet and his family, that when he saw the apparent motions of the spheres, and the reaction of the elements to the changes of the higher spheres and their changes of location and the differences of those bodies in terms of greatness, nobility and luminosity, he realizes that their originator, illuminator and agent of motion by

way of arousing desire and of assistance is not body
or corporeal, and said, "Lo. I have turned my face
toward Him Who created the heavens and the earth,
as one by nature upright, and I am not of the
polytheists (6:79)."[4]

In our view, the application of the above-mentioned verses [6:74-
79) to such a characteristic argument as seen in the wording of
Mulla Sadra does not seem to be very justified.

As can be seen from the different parts of the verses mentioned
above and especially from the conclusion, "... I am not from the
polytheists", they pertain to the Oneness of God, not to proving
the existence of God. However, they indirectly pertain to proving
the existence of the Creator, just through the need of the temporal
for the Everlasting, without appealing to the motions of the
spheres and getting involved in certain complicated discussions.

Is Knowledge of the existence of God Innate?

In doctrinal discussions, the point that is repeatedly made is that if
knowledge of God is not self-evident, at least, it is an innate
knowledge. In this regard, verse 30 of the Chapter named the
Romans is often mentioned. It says:

"So set thy purpose (O Muhammad) for religion as
a man by nature upright-the nature made by Allah,
in which He hath created man. There is no altering
(the laws of) Allah's creation. That is the right
religion, but most men know not." (30:30).

What Is Meant by Innateness?

In his *al-Mabda' wa'l-Ma'ad*, Mulla Sadra says in this regard:

'...nay, as has been already stated, [belief in] the
Necessary Being, the Exalted, is something innate,
because when man faces horrors and difficult

88

circumstances, by nature he puts his trust in God, the Exalted and turns instinctively to [the One Who is] the cause of causes and who eases difficulties even though he may not be aware of it and for this reason, it is seen that most Gnostics argue for the existence of God and His governance in regard to the creatures through the state in which man finds himself when such terrible things as drowning and burning occur.'[5]

In this discussion, Sardar al-muta'llhin mentions a number of Qur'anic verses in which man's tendency towards God and his taking refuge in Him in times of wretchedness are referred to. One verse that he mentions is:

"And when they mount upon the ships they pray to God, making their faith pure for Him only, but when He bringeth them safe to land, behold, they ascribe partners (unto him)." (29:65).

Verses 22 and 23 of the Chapter of Yunus (Jonah) and verse 32 of the Chapter Luqman also cover the same topic. However, a careful consideration of these verses shows that none of them pertains to proving the existence of God through primordial human nature. A close analysis of the above-mentioned verse shows that it is intended to make man aware of the falsehood of polytheism and the inability of the man-made gods to help him in times of danger. Therefore, while the verse deals with something innate, it does not pertain to the necessity of the [existence] of God, the Exalted, but rather it is about the Oneness of God and the falsehood of polytheism. As regards those who associate others with God (polytheists), who believe both in God, the Creator and in the false gods and who say that they should worship them so that they may help man in difficult circumstances, the above-mentioned verse is intended to awaken them to their original nature in order for them to discover the evident truth that the false gods can do nothing. The evidence for this truth is the innate reaction, which even the polytheists show

89

when they are confronted with certain critical situations. In those sensitive moments, they pray only to God, the Creator. So, why do they forget this truth? When they are saved from such situations, they go to the idol-temple, bow down to the idols and pray to them for help.

Verses 23 and 33 of the Chapter named Luqman mention man's forgetfulness of God and criticize him for being so ungrateful in times of ease and comfort and also for committing sins blatantly, without being worried that God may take away from him all the comfort and bounty he bestowed upon him and thereby punish him.

Also, verse 30 of the Chapter named the Romans, which considers the religion [of Islam] to be based upon the innate disposition as instilled by God in mankind, first refers to the very Oneness of God and to the fact that human original nature testifies to the falsehood of associating others with God (polytheism). [6]

A Covenant between Man and God: The World of Pre-existence

Verses 172 and 173 of the Chapter named A'rāf (*the Heights*) mention the covenant between man and God which is held by some Muslim authorities to pertain to the innateness of belief in God and His Oneness:

> "And (remember) when thy Lord brought forth from the children of Adam, from their reins, their seed, and made them testify of themselves, (saying), 'Am I not Lord?' They said, 'Yes, verily. We testify.' (That was) lest ye should say on the Day of Resurrection, 'Lo! of this we were unaware;'[7] Or lest ye should say, '(It is) only (that) our fathers ascribed partners to Allah of old and we were (their) seed after them. Wilt Thou destroy us on account of that which those follow falsehood did?'"

90

These verses mention the dialogue between God and all human beings, during which all of humanity spoke to God and testified to His Lordship and to His governance of the world of existence (the ordering and administering of the universe). It is testified by virtue of which any excuse made for being aware or unaware or being influenced by one's ancestors is rejected as unjustified on the Day of Resurrection.

The Scene of the Covenant [as portrayed in the Qur'an]

In the books of tradition and exegesis, we encounter various opinions about this matter.

In many traditions recounted about the Holy Prophet (peace be upon him), his companions, the early commentators and the Imams (peace be upon them all), there is the view that God gathered together all human beings descended from Adam in their pre-cosmic state of existence in the form of tiny particles. They testified to the Lordship of God in their pre-eternal ontological reality so that there might be no room left for any excuse made by anyone at any time or place.[8]

According to this view, special attention has been paid to the derivation of *dhuriyyah* (offspring) from *dharrah* (*atoms, tiny particles*), and the scene has been named the world of pre-existence (*'alam al-dharr*), that is, a world in which all human beings as tiny particles were all present together. Some of the modern Qur'anic commentators, such as Sayyid Qutb have given the example of genetics as supporting evidence in order to make it more understandable to the readers.[9] According to them, any human being in his own nature, or to put it differently, in his own original human nature (*fitrah*)[10] is aware of God and of His Oneness. He is born with the potentiality enough to possess this consciousness or in genetic parlance, he is born with the gene, which gives him the possibility of possessing this consciousness. This gene is always transmitted from one generation to the next and thus the potentiality to possess this consciousness is transmitted too. The genetic characteristics that exist in all human beings in a scattered form, exist in primitive man's genes in a concentrated form.

Hasan al-Basri (110-21AH) and many other commentators, particularly the Mu'tazilites, hold that from the [above-mentioned] verse, it is not understood that there is a world called the world of pre-existence in which all human beings were gathered in the form of tiny particles and made a covenant with their Lord. Rather, what the verse refers to is that God-seeking nature with which every human being is born, and when he reaches the stage of maturity and awareness, it will have developed into a clear concept of God in such a way that to the question: 'Am I not your Lord?' the answer which is given by every human being from within is, 'Yes, Indeed'. Therefore, according to these commentators, this verse does not refer to a specific event that took place between God and all human beings in the past history of humanity, but rather it speaks of an event beginning from the birth of every human being, which is the first stage of growth and consciousness and which precedes the following stages [of his growth and development]. Often, he is influenced by the corrupting factors of his environment and thus, the development and growth of his innate God-consciousness is stunted.[11]

Another View on the World of Pre-existence

`Allamah Tabatabai holds a different view on the scene mentioned in the verses quoted above.[12] According to him, all human beings and all other creatures that come into existence in a gradual manner are altogether present before God, who transcends time and space, because the gradual passage of time, and such temporal notions as today, yesterday and tomorrow are applied to us and other creatures that are within the bounds of time. Right now, we face something and a moment later, we are a moment away from it. A moment later, there are two moments interval between us and that thing. Tomorrow, the interval will be one day, and next year the interval will be one year long, and so on.

However, the passage of time, which lengthens our distance from the past and shortens our distance from the future, does not apply to God because God transcends time and space, and thus there is no spatio-temporal separation between Him and us.

With this view in mind, it follows that if all human beings, or rather all the creatures who are within the bounds of time, are present altogether with God, if the children of Adam were taken together with their ancestors and gathered in the presence of God, they would intuitively know their Creator and their knowledge would be clear evidence of the existence of God and His Lordship. However, being subject to the passage of time and the process of changes in the world of nature, keeps one so engaged and absorbed that one can become negligent of one's intuitive knowledge of God, the Creator and Lord. Such negligence seems to be the same as self-alienation, which has been brought up in many old and modern philosophical schools of thought, such as existentialism, as one of the critical problems of man's life on earth. Self-alienation as one of the serious problems [of modern man] that not only harms the self-consciousness of many of human beings and sometimes makes them completely unconscious of the self, but it also harms their God-consciousness. The problem may lead to such an extent that people may become blind to God despite his manifestness and become totally negligent of Him.

What has just been presented is a summary, with minor modifications, of what has been discussed in detail in *Al-Mizān*.

> 'There was a heedless person with whom God was at all times
>
> 'But he did not sense it and from afar kept calling on God.'[13]

In his detailed exposition, Allamah Tabatabai has dealt with the subject itself and with its relevance to the verse as extensively as possible and has given an adequate and fruitful explanation.

In spite of all this, it seems that the relevance of the verse to this subject needs still more interpretation. What can be said on the substance of this verse is that within it, a stage of man's existence is mentioned where man acknowledges the Lordship of God. The acknowledgement is not strong enough to keep human beings on the straight path of worshipping the One God forever, but it is effective enough to prepare their intellectual and intuitive readiness for seeking God, so that they may not make any excuses for being ignorant of this matter on the Day of Resurrection.

This innate readiness is so far-reaching that it can enable every human being to abandon the superstitious ideas of his ancestors and take the righteous path without making such excuses as: 'Our forefathers were polytheists and we followed in their footsteps'. However, as far as the characteristics of this stage, the stage at which a covenant was made between God and human beings, are concerned, no more details have been given in the Qur'an.

Love of God, Inclination towards God, and Seeking God out of love for Him also means the Natural Disposition [to Seek God] (*fitrah*)

Those who contemplate and possess a strong inner urge to seek the Ultimately Reality maintain that there is a different kind of relationship between man and God [out of love for Him]. This kind of relation can be interpreted as the natural disposition instilled by God in man. It consists in love of the Absolute [Reality], Absolute Being, Absolute Perfection, Absolute Good, and so on which can be found in every normal human being as a natural inclination. It is this very attraction that reminds him of God, who is Absolute Perfection, and draws his attention towards Him. Furthermore, the attraction becomes so strong within certain individuals that it will turn into love, joy and rapture, which thereby draws the attention of the God-centred man toward the transcendent world and awakens the love of God in his heart. According to the individuals who hold the view explained above, love of perfection and inclination toward absolute perfection exists even within the nature of those who deny the existence of God even if they may be unaware of this inner urge [to seek God].

Man is negligent and unaware of many strong inner desires, which lie hidden within his soul. Today, they are recognized by the experimental sciences and are also the main subject matter of one of the most fruitful branches of the modern human sciences, namely, psychoanalysis. Therefore, it is worth employing the most accurate results of this discipline to carry out an in-depth scientific study of various spiritual states in order to discover their real causes in a scientific manner. Thus, we will not rely upon the various unreliable views, which are mostly superficial and based on personal prejudices and preferences.

However, from the perspective of the Gnostics, if man pays more attention to his innate love of perfection and strengthens it through spiritual discipline, worship and prayer, finally he will attain the stage where he will find God, that is, the stage of intuition, which is accompanied with certainty. Finding and certainty will leave no room for doubt. From their point of view, the only certain path to know God is to seek God, which will ultimately lead to finding God. As the Qur'an explains when it addresses the Prophet in the following verse:

> "So proclaim that which thou art commanded, and withdraw from the idolaters. Lo! We defend thee from the scoffers, who set some other god along with Allah. But they will come to know. Well know we that thy bosom is at times oppressed by what they say, but hymn the praise of thy Lord, and be of those who make prostration (unto Him), and serve thy Lord till certainty[14] cometh unto thee." (15:94-99).

Therefore, praising, glorifying and worshipping are paths to attain certainty. The intuition and certainty that are attained by the Gnostics are something like the direct knowledge and certainty that man attains in regard to sense data. In the same way that sense experiences are the best means of removing fallacious doubts, [doubting the reality of] what we perceive, the best way to remove doubts about God is also to attain an immediate knowledge of Him. This is not acquired by sight but by insight, or spiritual vision. A Gnostic finds clearly through this vision that he is truly the lover of the Real and not a lover of an illusory beloved.

Knowledge of God is based on Innate Simple and Clear Perceptions

One of the other ways through which innate knowledge of God can be interpreted is that in order to know God, there is no need for complex arguments. For this reason, whenever the Qur'an argues [for the existence of God], it does no more than draw the attention of man to the simplest and clearest innate perceptions and request him to accept the necessary and undeniable results of these perceptions. In fact, in most cases, the Qur'an does not even appeal greatly to reasoning but confines itself to warning man against the illusory and false nature of an atheistic belief or tendency, and thereby encourages him to seek God more and more persistently, as it did with regards to the materialists[15] and the root-cause of their beliefs.

Becoming Aware of God's Existence through Reflection upon His Signs

In many of the verses, the Qur'an invites the wise, the thoughtful, the spiritually aware and so on, to reflect deeply on the universe and its marvels, even on the normal natural events and the causes of their occurrence, and thus come to know the All-Knowing, All-Powerful, All-Wise, and Merciful One God. These verses often seek to awaken man and to draw his attention to those issues which are raised after proving the Creator's existence, such as Oneness, Power, Infinite wisdom, and other Divine attributes, especially His power to resurrect men for an eternal life which is accompanied by the reward and punishment of their acts in this world. However, in all these verses, in order to understand the

96

unseen realities, man is invited to meditate on the signs of the manifest world by using his insight and innate perceptions so that he may understand thereby the supra-sensible realities and acquire useful and reliable knowledge of them.

In view of the above conclusion drawn from meditation on the visible signs, in order to understand the supra-sensible realities that are emphasized in these verses, the question posed is as follows:

If the universe and its various parts, from the smallest particles to the galaxies and from minerals to plants to man, are clear signs of knowledge, power, will, mercy, wisdom, and other attributes of the majesty and beauty of God, the Creator, are they not by themselves clear signs of the every existence of God, the Creator?

If the answer to this question is positive, we will conclude that although the Qur'an does not raise the question of proving the existence of God directly in view of the intellectual climate of the people it first faced, it adopts an approach which is fruitfully useable for proving the existence of God and also for acquiring clear and reliable knowledge of His existence when raising other questions that follow the question of proving the existence of God. The main support of this approach is to pay attention to the individual needs of the phenomena of this universe and to its independent Creator, who possesses enough power to create wonderful creatures. The essential dependence and needs of the creatures are clear evidence of the existence of that independent Being, and attention to the ephemeral nature of each of them is clear evidence of their dependency on a self-subsistent Being.

Verses 15-17 of the Chapter named *al-Fatir* (*The Originator*) may pertain to the total need of man for God and to the doctrinal conclusions that are drawn from it:

> "O mankind! Ye are the poor in your relations to Allah. And Allah, He is the Absolute, the owner of praise, If He will, He can be rid of you and bring

(instead of you) some new creation. That is no a hard thing for Allah." (35:15-17).

Therefore, it can be said with regards to the way in which God's attributes can be known, the Qur'an presents a way to man that can also be used for proving the existence of God.

Endnotes

1. *Al-Mizan*, vol. 12, pp. 2-3

2. Translator's note: Socrates' major philosophical method was that of *elenchus* (cross-examination, refutation): eliciting and questioning of beliefs in order to establish truths and reveal inconsistencies.

3. Translator's note: Natural motion is one which results from the nature of an object and which does not need an outward force in order to occur. For example: Heavy bodies naturally move toward the centre of the earth, therefore falling is a natural motion. The natural motion of objects is one of the characteristics of an object. For example: The natural movement of the celestial bodies made of ether is circular.

Violent motion, by contrast, is motion contrary to the nature of the object and requires an external force in order to occur. Most motions are of this type. A stone thrown into the air moves in a violent motion, against its nature and therefore requires force in order to cause it to move.

Although Galileo rejected Aristotle's theory, he learned a great deal from the books of Aristotle and his school, and even preserved some of the Aristotelian concepts, most of which were subsequently abandoned by modern science.

4. *Al-Mabda' wa'l-Ma'ad*, Edited with prolegomena and notes by Sayyid Jalal al-Din Ashtiyani, Persian and English Introductions by Seyyed Hossein Nasr, Tehran, 1976, pp. 17-18. It should be noted that the quotations from *al-Mabda' wa'l-Ma'ad* have been translated by the translator from Arabic into English.

5. Ibid. p. 23.

6. Allamah Tabatabai holds a more comprehensive view while commenting on the verse on the innateness of religion, and he

holds that all the religious teachings [of Islam] are congruous with all the natural needs of man within the framework of a solid system of belief and action.

7. Tanslator's Note: In verses 172-173, the issue of faith and human nature as described in a very vivid scene shows the pre-cosmic existence of the generations of the distant future, as they are still in the loins of human beings and no bigger than small atoms held in the hand of the great Lord, before they make their appearance in this visible world. All of them are gathered in front of their Creator who asks them: "Am I not your Lord?" As rational beings, They replied: "Yes, indeed, we bear witness to that," (Verse: 172) on account of the inner qualities placed by God in them, acknowledging His Lordship, admitting their position as obedient servants and His status as the only Lord and giving their pledges when they are still in the loins of their ancestors.

It is worth noting that in Verse 172, by "they" is meant all the children of Adam, and by "yes" the affirmation of God's Oneness by us in our pre-eternal ontological status. Men and women still bear the echo of the "yes" deeply embedded in their souls, and the message of Islam is precisely addressed to this primordial nature.

8. See Fakhr al-Din al-Razi, *Tafsir al-Kabir,* vol. 15, pp. 46-49, al-Tabarsi, *Majma' al-Bay'ān*, vol. 4, pp. 497-498, al-Tabatabai, *op. cit.*, vol. 8, pp. 338-346

9. See, for example, al-Sayid Qutb, *Fi Ûilāl al-Qur'an*, vol. 3, p. 670

10. Translator's note: The term *fitra* is commonly translated as "primordial nature" or "innate disposition". Its root meaning, which is to split or to cleave, implies opening up and coming out. The verb also means to bring forth and to originate, and in everyday language, to knead and to shape dough. The word *fit'ra* itself is employed only once in the Qur'an, along with the verb

form of the word in 3:30, according to which every person is born with a pure primordial nature and innately recognizes the Oneness of God.

11. See al-Tabarsi, *op. cit.*, vol. 4, p. 498, al-Razi, *op.cit.*, vol. 15, pp. 46-52

12. Al-Tabatabai, *op.cit.*, vol. 8, pp. 329-336

13. This is a verse of poetry quoted by the writer.

14. Certainty means clear and unambiguous knowledge. Immediate knowledge is the best type of certain knowledge, and the area of action is the most appropriate ground for acquiring it, as it is in this area that man can acquire the opportunity to face every type of objective reality and not to be drowned in one's subjective ideas, ones which most often are totally far removed from objective reality and which prevent man from comprehending reality.

15. *Surah al-Jāthiyah (Kneeling)*: 24

The Ontological Argument in Islamic Metaphysics

Dr Karim Aghili

The ontological argument or rather the proof of the truthful (*burhān al-ṣiddiqin*) as explained by Ibn Sina and Mulla Sadra is one of the most convincing proofs for the existence of God in comparison to those put forward by their predecessors. This argument has certain features that distinguish it from other arguments, such as the argument from necessity and contingency, the argument from temporal origination and so on. In this paper, I will study different versions of the ontological argument and conclude that Allamah Tabataba'i's version has certain advantages over the other ones, because, apart from its concision, it relies upon the absoluteness and eternal necessity of pure existence.

The Ontological Argument in Western Philosophy

In the western philosophy of religion, the ontological argument which purports to rationally prove the existence of God from the concept of God as a supremely perfect being, was first expounded by St. Anselm in his *Proslogion* and *Response to Gaunilo,* though it was Kant, who first called the argument "ontological." John Duns Scotus, St. Thomas Aquinas, Rene Descartes, Baruch Spinoza, Gottfried Leibinz and Immanuel Kant, have all made their own major contributions to the ontological arguments in their various versions. Furthermore, in the twentieth century, we see major contributions made by such figures as Charles Hartshorne, Norman Malcom, James Ross and Alvin Plantinga. Some believe that the ontological argument as used by Anselm and some others should be called a "modal" argument, because it relies on such modal concepts as possibility, actuality, and necessity.

This paper will deal mainly with the ontological argument in Islamic metaphysics. Therefore, it will not be possible to deal with all the different versions of the ontological argument in western metaphysics within the scope of this article. Instead, I wish to deal with the two versions of the ontological argument as advanced by St. Anselm in the sixteenth century. Succinct as it is, it seems to be the quintessence of all ontological arguments in the Western philosophy of religion.

Anselm's First Version of the Ontological argument

The ontological argument is of a purely *a priori* or analytic nature because it does not appeal to any facts of experience, but it is concerned with existence as part of the definition of God and that therefore God must exist. As mentioned earlier, the ontological argument was first originated by Anselm (1033-1109). In Chapter 2 of his *Proslogion*, Anselm defines God as 'that than which nothing greater can be conceived'. Such an idea also exists in the mind of those who deny God's existence. An example of this is the fool mentioned in Psalms 14:1, who says in his heart there is no God. However, if the concept exists only in the mind, it fails to be 'that than which nothing greater can be conceived' as it would be inferior to that which exists in reality. Therefore, 'that than which nothing greater can be conceived' cannot exist only in the mind but it must also exist in reality. Anselm writes:

> '[Even a] fool, when he hears of...a being than which nothing greater can be conceived...understands what he hears, and what he understands is in his understanding...And assuredly that, than which nothing greater can be conceived, cannot exist in the understanding alone. For suppose it exists in the understanding alone, then it can be conceived to exist in reality; which is greater...Therefore, if that, than which nothing greater can be conceived, exists in the

understanding alone, the very being, than which nothing greater can be conceived, is one, than which a greater can be conceived. But obviously this is impossible. Hence, there is no doubt that there exists a being, than which nothing greater can be conceived, and it exists both in the understanding and in reality.'[1]

Anselm's Second Version of the Ontological Argument

There are two different versions of the ontological argument in the *Prosologion*. Most of the arguments in *Proslogion* Chapter 2 are logically distinct, though very similar, from what is presented in Chapter 3.

In Chapter 3 of *Proslogion*, Anselm argues that, although a person can be thought of as non-existent, the same is not true of God: He exists necessarily. This is because, if God did not exist necessarily, he would not be 'that than which nothing greater can be conceived'.

The second version of the argument does not claim that existence is a property. Instead, it relies on the claim that *necessary* existence is perfection. In other words, if something cannot be thought of as non-existent, then such a thing would be greater than something that can be thought of as non-existent. That is, the thing whose non-existence is *logically impossible* is greater than that whose non-existence is logically possible. Here is the second version of the ontological argument as Anselm states it:

> 'God is that than which nothing greater can be conceived...And [God] assuredly exists so truly, that He cannot be conceived not to exist. For, it is possible to conceive of a being that cannot be conceived not to exist; and this is greater than one that can be conceived not to exist. Hence, if that, than which nothing greater can be conceived, can be conceived not to exist, it is not that, than which nothing greater can be conceived. But this is an irreconcilable

contradiction. There is, then, so truly a being than which nothing greater can be conceived to exist, that it cannot even be conceived not to exist; and this being thou art, O Lord, our God.'[2]

It is important to note that Anselm uses 'necessary' in a sense different from that used by Aquinas in his Third Way. In the Third Way, God's necessity means that He is not dependent on anything else. For Anselm, however, something exists necessarily if its non-existence would be self-contradictory. Necessity of this kind is often called logical necessity.

At this point, it would be appropriate to contrast logical necessity, or essential necessity with eternal necessity. Essential necessity is that in which the affirmation of a predicate of its subject depends upon the continuance of the existence of its subject. In other words, the predicate is affirmed of the subject as long as the subject exists. Eternal necessity is that in which the predicate is affirmed of its subject unconditionally.

The Ontological Argument in Islamic Metaphysics

Many arguments have been cited for the existence of God in Islamic theology and philosophy, among which the ontological argument, that is the argument of the truthful, holds a special place. In this argument, it is not the contingents that are used to prove the existence of God; rather it is existence itself that is demonstrated by existence. However, the other arguments proceed from the contingent being to the Necessary Being (God). Normally, the Muslim theologians argue for the existence of God from temporal origination. However, the argument from contingency and necessity refers to the procedure of arguing from the contingency of created beings, and the argument from causality relies upon creatures as effects.

The question that is posed at this point is whether the universe and the creatures within it should be used as a middle term to argue for the existence of God, or the world should be considered manifest and God non-manifest, that is, hidden. Or perhaps it is not necessary that we should pose this question because these types of arguments are exclusive to those who lack a high degree of intellectual understanding and who have not come to possess spiritual insight?

In Islamic metaphysics in its specific sense, there is a discussion to the effect that while God is non-manifest, He is manifest and while He is manifest, He is non-manifest. According to the Qur'an,

> "He is the First and the Last, the Manifest and the Hidden." (57: 3)

In this verse, it is the divine essence that demonstrates His essence and unity. Imam Ali (as) says in the Supplication for the Morning:

> 'Oh He who has demonstrated His Essence by His Essence'[3]

Imam Ali (as) also says in Sermon 64 in *the Nahj al-Balaghah*:

> 'Every manifest thing other than Him is not non-manifest, and every non-manifest thing other than Him is not manifest.'[4]

Also in Sermon 186 he says:

> 'His non-manifestation does not hide His manifestation and His manifestation does not prevent Him from nonmanifestation'.[5]

Similarly, in Sermon 162 he says:

> 'He is manifest, but it cannot be said "from what". He is nonmanifest, but it cannot be said "in what".'[6]

Imam Husayn (as) says in *Prayer for the Day of Arafah*:

'How can You be demonstrated by that which is in need of You for its existence? Can anything other than You be self-manifesting so that it may manifest You, while You are [self-manifesting]. When have You ever been hidden so that You may need a proof that demonstrates You, and when have You ever been distant so that You may be sought by the signs which lead to You.'[7]

It has been proved in the transcendent theosophy of Mulla Sadra that the aspects of manifestation and non-manifestation are identical in the Divine Essence. That is to say, He does not possess two aspects, one of which is manifest and the other non-manifest. He possesses a single aspect, which is at once the origin of manifestation and that of non-manifestation. The single aspect consists in the absolute actuality and infinite intensity of existence. As Hajji Mulla Sabziwari has said:

'Oh He who is hidden due to the extremity of His light

Oh manifest One who is non-manifest due to His manifestation.'[8]

To give a brief explanation, it has been proved in Islamic metaphysics that the Pure Essence of God, the Exalted, is hidden because of the intensity of self-manifestation. In order to become more familiar with this matter, we will put forward three premises:

1. In the same way that existence is of two modes: existence in itself (objective existence) and existence for others (mental existence), manifestation is also of two types: manifestation in itself and manifestation for others. Therefore, when we discuss manifestation or non-manifestation, we sometimes refer to the

manifestation of a thing in itself and sometimes we refer to the manifestation of a thing for others.

2. It has been proved in Muslim metaphysics that existence is synonymous with manifestation, and non-manifestation is derived from non-existence. An existent partakes of manifestation to the same degree that it partakes of existence, and it is devoid of manifestation to the same degree that the deficiency is mixed with and pervades its existence. So, an existent that is of the highest and most perfect of existence is of the highest and most perfect of manifestation.

3. There is no correlation between two modes of manifestation, that is, it is not the case that if anything in itself is of the highest degree of manifestation, its manifestation for others should necessarily be of the highest degree. Rather, the opposite is true to some extent, because the manifestation of a thing for others depends on the nature of the structure of our sensory faculties.

Our sensory faculties have been created in such a way that they can only perceive and reflect within themselves the entities that are confined and limited within the bounds of time and space and which also possess the characteristics of opposition and similarity. Our senses perceive colours, shapes, sounds and others things, because they are limited temporally and spatially. For example, we perceive whiteness, because it exists somewhere and does not exists somewhere else. It exists at times and does not exist at other times. If there were whiteness everywhere, we would never recognize whiteness, and would have no concept of whiteness within our minds. We come to know of the existence of light, because it is sometimes present and sometimes not present, and present somewhere and not present somewhere else. If there were no shadow and darkness, light would not have been recognized. If the world were uniformly lit, we would never know of light, that is, the very thing in whose light we see everything.

Mahmud Shabistari, the renowned Persian mystic says in this regard in his *Gulshan-i-Rāz* (*the Rose Garden of Divine Mysteries*):

'Fool that he is! for he seeks the blazing sun

By the dim light of a torch in the desert.

If the sun tarried always in one position,

And if his shining were all after one manner,

None would know these beams are from him,

There would be no distinction between kernel and husk [the disc of the sun and its light],

Know that the whole is a beam of the light of "The Truth",

Yet "the Truth" within it is concealed from manifestation;

And since the light of "The Truth" alters not nor varies,

And is void of change and transitoriness.'[9]

The same is the case with sounds. If we always heard a sound uniformly, we would never hear it. Things are known by their opposites.

Based on the explanation of the above three premises, it can be said that the Divine essence is Pure Being and Pure Actuality, and is totally free from potentiality. In terms of manifestation, He is the very manifestation, and there is no aspect of non-manifestation within Him. However, in terms of manifestation, such is not the case. The very perfection of His manifestation is the source of His non-manifestation, because He is existentially unlimited, and He is Omnipresent and with everything, and nothing, no place and no moment are void of him but not in the sense of incarnation or union. This is the reason why our limited senses, our sensory faculties, cannot perceive Him.

The perfection of manifestation of the Divine essence and the infinitude of His existence mean that His being is hidden from us. This is the meaning of the first line of the above-mentioned verse. God is hidden due to the extremity of manifestation and this is the message relayed in the words of the Muslim philosophers. The aspects of manifestation and non-manifestation within the Divine essence are one and the same. It is not the case that part of His existence is manifest and another is non-manifest. He has no parts at all, and His whole existence is at once manifest and non-manifest.

The Muslim 'urafa (gnostics) strictly criticise the philosophers for proving the existence of God through creatures and for considering the universe manifest and God non-manifest. Rumi, the renowned mystic Persian and sage, also says in this regard:

> 'The proof of the sun is the sun (himself);
>
> If thou require the proof, do not avert thy face from him!
>
> If the shadow gives an indication of him,
>
> The sun (himself) gives spiritual light every moment.
>
> The shadow, like chat in the night-hours, brings sleep to thee;
>
> When the sun rises the moon is cloven asunder.'
> (Nicholson Translation)

Junaid of Baghdad was once asked: What is the proof for the existence of the Creator? In reply, he said: The light of daybreak makes the light of a lamp redundant.[10]

The Originator of the Ontological Argument in Islamic Metaphysics

Among the philosophers, Ibn Sina (Avicenna) is the first to have employed the ontological argument for the existence of God. In his own way, he employed an argument in which he did not appeal to creatures to prove the existence of God. As is understood from the words of Ibn Sina, this type of argument was not present among the earlier philosophers. Of course, Ibn Sina as well as Mulla Sadra and a number of the later Muslim philosophers specify explicitly that a number of the Qur'anic verses indicate this method.

After expounding his version of the argument, Ibn Sina goes on to say:

> 'Consider carefully how our exposition for proving the First and His Unity and His transcending all flaws does not need thinking about other than existence itself, and there is no need for considering His creation and Act even though that [path] might [also] be [another] proof of Him, but this path is more trustworthy and nobler. That is, when we consider the state of existence, existence qua existence attests to the necessary and after that, it testifies to His attributes, and in the Divine Book, a reference has been made to such a point: "Soon We shall show them Our signs in the horizons and in their own souls until it becomes clear to them that He is the Real." I believe that this is a judgement for certain people. Then, He says: "Is it not sufficient that your Lord is witness to all things?" (41:51). I assert that this is a judgement for the truthful who testify [from Him] to Him not [from that which is other than Him] to Him.'[11]

An Explanation of the Version of Ibn Sina

Existence is either necessary or contingent. If it were necessary, the object is proved and if it were contingent, it must lead to the necessary in order for it not to become a vicious circle or an infinite series.

The Features of this Version are as follows:

111

1. This argument does not need to consider the attributes of creatures unlike the *a posteriori* (empirical arguments), such as the argument from temporal beginning, the argument from motion and the argument from the soul. These arguments deal with the attributes of creatures and prove temporal beginning, motion and so on, because in the *a posteriori* arguments, some of the premises are derived from the natural sciences. However, this version is of a totally philosophical nature and all its premises are derived from metaphysics in its general sense, the subject matter of which is existence qua existence.

2. It is worth noting that this version does not need to prove the existence of creatures because its first premise is formulated in the form of an assumption.

The premises used for forming the argument are as follows:

a) In this argument, the principle of the existence of reality has been taken as indubitable and self-evident. Denial of this premise is regarded as sophistry or scepticism. The principle of the reality of existence cannot be denied or doubted at all. Man accepts his own existence and ideas, and this very acceptance is assumed as accepting objective reality and existence.

b) Existence is divided into the Necessary Being and the contingent being and this division as a rational division is of a restrictive nature. Existence is either necessary or contingent, and there is no third alternative conceivable other than this. The division revolves around affirmation and negation. The existence of an existent being is either necessarily essential to and inseparable from it, as for example, evenness is inseparable from the number ten, and this is called the Necessary Being; or the existence of an existent being is not essentially necessary and its essence is indifferent to existence and non-existence and separable from it. Such an existent is called a contingent existent.

This premise is self-evident; if it is properly understood, it cannot be doubted. It is so evident that it needs no argument.

c) Every contingent needs an existentiating (existence–giving) cause, because based upon the definition given of the contingent being, its essence is equal to existence and non-existence, and existence is not a necessity. As long as the existentiating cause has not brought it out of non-existence, it will not come into existence. Thus, every contingent needs an existentiating cause for actualisation.

Although this premise is clear and needs no proof, in Islamic philosophy, there are certain arguments that have been given for it, and they can be considered an aid for further illustration. However, the premise is self-evident.

d) The vicious circle and the infinite regress are impossible.

The impossibility of the vicious circle is self-evident. If the subject and predicate are properly understood, the conclusion that a vicious circle and an infinite regress are impossible will be rationally affirmed. The vicious circle means that one existent being in relation to another existent being is at the same time, both a cause and an effect. It is clear from this though, that the cause implies needlessness and the effect implies need. The co-existence of needlessness and need at the same time entails contradiction.

However, the impossibility of an infinite regress is of a speculative nature and needs to be proved. Numerous proofs have been offered, some of which indicate the impossibility of an infinite regress with respect to all real things, covering actual existents arranged in successive order. Others consider an infinite regress to be impossible only with respect to real, efficient causes. An investigation of the proofs offered in this respect should be sought in its appropriate place, in metaphysics under the heading of causality.

Based on the above premises, the argument of Ibn Sina can be explained as follows:

The principle of existence or reality is the dividing line between philosophy and sophistry. Any intelligent person affirms the principle of existence and reality, and accepts that there are certain realities. At least, he affirms his existence, mind and ideas. The questions that can be posed are: is this reality necessary? That is, is its existence necessary and inseparable? If not, is it contingent? There is no third alternative conceivable, as dividing existence into the necessary being and the contingent being is restrictive. If the answer to the former question is positive, the object, that is, the Necessary Being, has been proved. If, however, it is the case that existence is not necessary but contingent and, as has been said, the contingent being is indifferent to existence and non-existence, the question then arises as to what cause or preponderating factor has brought it out of non-existence into existence. Were the contingent being by itself capable of emerging from this state of indifference, it would mean that the contingent being was the cause of its own existence and this would lead to a vicious circle. If there is another cause or preponderating factor, let us then move the argument to consider it and ask: Is this other cause necessary or contingent? If it is necessary, the object is proved, but if it is contingent, let us then move the argument to its cause or preponderating factor, and so, finally, in order for an infinite regress not to occur, the series of causes must lead to a Necessarily Existent Being.

Through this argument, it is proved that there is a Necessarily Existent Being. However, only the principle of existence is proved through this, but the attributes of the Necessary Being are left untouched. Questions such as: is the Necessary Being corporeal or not? Is It one or many, simple or composite? Does It have such attributes of perfection like knowledge or power? And what is the relationship between Its Essence and Its Attributes? These and other similar questions are all posed in metaphysics in its special sense, and finally through a host of arguments, it is proved that the Necessary Being is not corporeal but rather It is one and simple, and possesses all the attributes of perfection, and His attributes of essence are identical with His Essence.

Ibn Sina takes much pride in this mode of exposition and demonstration because it was unprecedented among his predecessors, and it is fair to say that his argument is of an original nature. However, Mulla Sadra does not consider this version an ideal one, because despite the fact that creatures are not used as the middle term in this argument. In one respect, it seems to be similar to the argument from temporal origination as it is put forward by the Muslim theologians and the argument from motion as put forward by the naturalists. The reason is that contingency, which is one of the properties of that constitutes the real nature of things, has been used as the middle term.

Mulla Sadra does not count the Ibn Sinian version among the versions of the proof of the truthful and tries to develop a new version of it. However, the fact that Ibn Sina has placed emphasis on the concept of existence makes his argument closer to the proof of the truthful than the arguments developed by his predecessors. In the path of the truthful, the focus is the reality of existence and not its concept. In this path, God is demonstrated by existence itself, and by His essence His attributes are demonstrated and by His attributes, His acts are demonstrated. The others seek access to that which is other than the reality of existence, such as whatish contingency, the generation of creatures, motion of the body, and so on.

In the Epilogue to *Kitāb al-Mashā'ir* (*The Book of Metaphysical Penetrations*), Mulla Sadra refers to a proof, which he calls the proof of the truthful (*burhan al-ṣidiqin*):

> 'Know that the paths towards God, the Exalted, are multiple, because He possesses innumerable excellences and aspects. "Everyone has a direction to which he turns." (2:148) However, some of these paths are more luminous, nobler, more rigorous and can be more cogently demonstrated. The most trustworthy and noblest of them leading to Him, His attributes and acts, is that in which the middle term of

demonstration is no other than Himself. Therefore, the path [entails] going to the object of the quest from the object of the quest, because He is the proof for all things. This is the path of all the Prophets and the Sincere, May God's peace be upon them all. "Say: This is my way. I call to Allah, I and those who follow me being certain, and glory be to Allah, and I am not one of the polytheists." (12:108) "This is indeed in the former scriptures, the scriptures of Abraham and Moses." (87:18-19) Thus, this [group] are those who attest to Him, the Exalted, through Him. "Allah bears witness that there is no God but He." (3:18) Then, they attest to His attributes through His Essence, then (attest to) His attributes, and from His attributes to His acts and effects, one after the other.

'Others seek to make their way towards the knowledge of God and of His attributes through what is other than Him. All the philosophers seek access to Him through the contingency of things, the naturalists through the motion of the body and the theologians through the temporality of created things and so forth. These are also proofs and evidences; however, the former path is stronger and nobler. The Divine Book alludes to those paths and He, Exalted be He, says, "Soon We shall show them Our signs in the horizons and in their souls until it becomes manifest unto them that He is the Real" (41:53), and he alluded to this path when He said, "Is it not sufficient that your Lord is a Witness to all things? " ' (41:53)[12]

It is worth noting that Sadra means Ibn Sina where he says,

'The philosophers seek access to Him through the contingency of things...'

116

The Version of Mulla Sadra in the *Asfar*

'The paths towards God are multiple, for He possesses innumerable excellences and aspects. And for every one is a direction to which he turns. However, some paths are more trustworthy, nobler and more illuminating than the other ones, and the strongest and the noblest of demonstrations in relation to Him is in fact that in which nothing other than Him is the middle term. Therefore the path towards the desired object is itself the very desired object, and it is the path of the sincere who attest to Him, the Exalted, through Him, and then they attest to His attributes through His Essence, and to His acts through His attributes one after the other, and others (such as the theologians, naturalists) seek to know Him, the Exalted and His attributes by adopting a path other than that [adopted by the sincere] (such as the contingency of the essence, the temporal beginning of creation, the motion of bodies and so on). They are also proofs for His Essence and provide evidence of His attributes. However, the former is stronger and nobler. A reference was made in the Divine Book to that [the former] path as He says,

"Soon We shall show them Our signs in the horizons and in their own souls until it becomes clear to them that He is the Real, and in reference to this [the latter] path, He says: Is it not sufficient that your Lord is witness to all things?" (41:51).

As has been said, existence is a single simple objective reality, between whose individuals there is no essential difference save in perfection and deficiency, strength and weakness or in additional matters [as has been said regarding the instances of specific essences (mahiyyah naw'iyyah)], and there is

117

nothing more complete than its ultimate perfection, and it is that which depends upon no other than itself, and nothing is conceived of that is more complete than it, because every imperfect thing relies on something other than itself, and is in need of all of its completion and it has already been made clear that the complete is prior to the imperfect, actuality prior to potentiality, and existence prior to non-existence, and it is also clear that the completion of a thing is that very thing and what is additional to it. Therefore, existence is either needless of other than itself or it is essentially in need of other than itself. The first one is the Necessary Being and It is the Pure Being and there is nothing more complete than it. Non-existence and imperfection are not mingled with it. The second is Its acts and effects, which are other than It and nothing other than It can subsist except through It. This is because, as mentioned earlier, the reality of existence is free from imperfection and if deficiency occurs, it is in virtue of its being an effect because the caused cannot be equal to the cause in virtue of existence. Therefore, if existence were not made by a dominant power that brings it into existence and actualises it (as it requires), it would not be conceivable that it would have any sort of deficiency, because the reality of existence is simple, indefinable, indeterminate, except for pure actuality and obtainment. Otherwise, it would be composite or it would have an essence other than being existent (mawjūdiyyah). As has already been said, if existence were caused, it would be made itself by the kind of making that is simple. Its essence by itself is in need of a maker, and it substantially and essentiality depends on its Maker.

Therefore, it has been proved and clarified that existence is either a complete reality and necessary in its selfhood, or it is essentially in need of [the

Necessary Being]. Substantiality depends on it and is based on each of the two divisions. We have therefore proven that the Necessary Being is in itself needless of what is other than this is what we have intended.'[13]

An Explanation of the Version of Mulla Sadra

The argument of the truthful is a proof for the existence of God that proceeds from the reality of existence to its eternal necessity. In this proof, the argument proceeds from existence to existence, and the path is the same as the object of desire. In the other proofs, the argument proceeds from creatures to the Creator, from contingency to necessity, from the created to the Creator, or from the subject of motion to the agent of motion. In this argument nothing save God is the middle term.

Thus, Mulla Sadra's version of the 'proof of the truthful', without relying on contingency or the falsity of a vicious circle, is based on two distinctive features of existence. These two features, which underlie Mulla Sadra's argument and are considered to be its two premises, consist of the principality or fundamentality of existence and the unity of the reality of existence.

In order to understand Mulla Sadra's argument, we should take into consideration certain principles, some of which are self-evident and others that are quasi-evident.

1. Distinction between the concept and the reality of existence. According to Mulla Sadra, there are two levels of reference with respect to existence: the conceptual level and the level of reality. Mulla Sadra makes a distinction between the concept of existence and the reality of existence. The concept of existence, which is self-evident, is of a mental nature. It is also of an irreducible nature, while all the other concepts are reduced to it. In contrast, the reality of existence, which is of an extra-mental nature, is the most difficult to understand or define. Existence as such, which is independent of all objects or existents, is beyond human understanding. As Hajji Mulla Hadi Sabziwari says:

'Its notion is one of the best-known things, but its deepest reality is in the extremity of hiddenness.'[14]

2. The Fundamentality of existence. Fundamentality of existence means that essences are mental constructs of a subjective nature and, by contrast, existence is the only extra-mental reality and actualisation itself. The unity of the reality of existence as the second premise that based on the fundamentality of existence and on the doctrine of the gradation of existence, consists of the fact that first, existence is a single fundamental reality, which is essentially one.

Second, the reality of existence consists of degrees and is graded and whatever exists are the levels and manifestations of existence, that is, the unity of existence and the multiplicity of existents. At this point, it is worth noting that the graded unity of existence based on the transcendent theosophy of Mulla Sadra contrasts with the view that existence consists of entities essentially disparate or disparate in their entirety, from each other, as held by the Peripatetic and with the individual unity of existence as espoused by the Gnostics ('urafā).

Third, existence has no second. In other words, existence in its absoluteness does not yield to reduplication or repetition. Thus, no fundamental reality except existence is conceivable. Based on the two premises put forth, it can be concluded that the single fundamental reality of existence is either essentially independent of the other or dependent on the other. The first assumption, the necessity of existence, is our object of desire and the point is proved through accepting it. The second assumption, the dependence of existence, means that its acceptance is tantamount to accepting that existence subsists through something else. This assumption is not consistent with the second assumption, because in conformity with the latter, existence has no second and in the domain of existence, there is no reality conceivable except the single reality of existence. Furthermore, other than existence, there is no reality conceivable, and other than existence, there is no second to the existence of the Real apart from the loci of manifestations of this very existence of the Real, and they are the very need and dependence. Therefore, the second assumption is false, and existence is the single fundamental reality of the Necessary Being. Thus, based on Mulla Sadra's doctrine of the fundamentality of existence, first, the Necessary Being is proved, and then, based on this very existence of the Necessary Being, the existence of contingents as the loci of manifestation of the existence of the Real is proved, and hence, the meanings of the Qur'anic verses mentioned above have been clarified.

Another Explanation of the Version of Mulla Sadra

Given that the fundamentality of existence, the graded unity of existence, and causality are the premises, the proof of the truthful can be formulated in accordance with the taste of Sadra al-muta'allihin as follows:

Existence is a single simple objective reality, the difference among whose individuals results from perfection and imperfection, and intensity and weakness. The highest level of that reality is the most complete, and the main characteristic of that level is absolute independence. The other levels are the very relation and dependence. Therefore, the reality of existence is of two kinds: that which is independent, and that which is the relation itself and poverty and need.

If the highest level did not exist, the other levels would not occur either. Otherwise the dependent and relative levels would be independent and without need, whereas they are the very relation and need. The deficiency and need of those levels is due to their being caused, by effects. The essence of the effect is the very relation and dependence. It is not the case that it is composed of an essence and a relation but rather the very essence is the relation. On the other hand, if a being were not caused, it would be free of deficiency and impotence, as the reality of existence qua existence. Existence regarded in its absoluteness and perfection is simple and it is not limited and determinate. It is pure actuality, otherwise it would be composite or it would have an essence other than existence.

Therefore, this proof has some advantages over the proof of Ibn Sina, because in this proof, there is no need for the refutation of a vicious circle or infinite regress.

What is emphasized in this proof is the reality of existence not the concept of existence. Therefore no mention is made of essential contingency, which is a rational attribute of the essence. Existence precedes the essence. What are emphasized in this proof are existential independence and dependence or needlessness and need.

A Symbolic Logic Approach to the Proof of the Truthful

Symbolic logic can provide us with a formal proof. A formal proof formulated in symbolic logic can only show the argument to be *valid*. An inference is valid if it is impossible for its premises to be true and its conclusion to be false. A valid argument is not necessarily sound. A *sound* argument is that which is both valid and that all its premises are true. An argument is *invalid* if it is possible that its premises are true but its conclusion is false.

With this view in mind, a version of the proof of the truthful using symbolic logic can be formulated as follows:

1. Existence necessarily exists = p

2. Existence contingently exists =q

3. Existence either necessarily or contingently exists = p v q

If it is the case that existence contingently exists, the contingent existent entails the Necessary Being, because unless there is a Necessarily existent Being, the contingent being will not be actualised.

122

4. $q \rightarrow p$

The combination of the two above premises, viz. **3** and **4,** results as follows:

5. $(p \lor q) \& (q \rightarrow p)$

At this point, an implication, that is, a conditional statement, is formulated and p, that is, the Necessary Being, becomes the consequence:

6. $[(p \lor q) \& (q \rightarrow p)] \rightarrow p$

Now the argument of the Truthful can be formalised in the following truth- table in which 1 stands for true and 0 stands for false:

P	q	p $\lor$ q	q $\rightarrow$ p	[(p $\lor$ q) &(q $\rightarrow$ p)]	$\rightarrow$ p
1	1	0	1	0	1
1	0	1	1	1	1
0	1	1	0	0	1
0	0	0	1	0	1

The above version can be explained as follows: Existence is either a necessary being or a contingent being. If it is the case that existence necessarily exists, the point is proved. However, if it is the case that existence contingently exists, the meaning of the

Necessary Being is contained within the nature of the contingent being. The contingent being thus implies the Necessary Being.[15]

On the other hand, it seems that the above-mentioned argument itself needs to be complemented and that a premise such as the impossibility of a vicious circle or an infinite regress is needed for its completion. The argument seems to be in the last analysis the same as that of Ibn Sina. For this reason, this version of the argument, which uses mathematical logic is problematic. How can it be the case that the contingent being itself implies the Necessary Being, while no proof has been given for it? Is there such a logical entailment between the concepts of the contingent and necessary beings or between the reality and instances of the contingent and necessary beings? If the first alternative is implied, how can it be proved merely through the logical entailment or necessity between the concepts that this very rule applies to their instances extra-mentally? Philosophical eternal necessity is that which cannot be inferred from logical concepts. This version is an instance of the confusion of concept and existence and if by existence the reality of existence is meant, what reason leads one to adopt this rule? Does an analysis of the meaning of the extra-mental contingent being, prove that a Necessary Being exists extra-mentally? Without appealing to the impossibility of a vicious circle or an infinite series, the argument will bear no fruit, because it will not be possible to prove through the logical entailment or logical necessity between the concepts of necessity and contingency that the rule applies extra-mentally.

The incompleteness of this version of the argument using mathematical logic, as given by Dr. Ha'iri Yazdi in his *Hiram-i Hasti* (*The Pyramid of Existence*), does not detract from the other arguments. The version of Mulla Sadra given above is of a totally strong and sound nature and does not appeal to mathematical logic, though it has been expounded based on conventional Aristotelian logic.

Another Version of Mulla Sadra's

In the *Asrar al-Ayāt*, Mulla Sara gives another version of the ontological argument as follows:

'The nature of absolute existence qua absolute is the reality of the Necessary Itself. The Exalted, and nothing other than the First Truth is the reality of existence itself, because that which is other than It is either an essence or an imperfect existence mixed with imperfection, deficiency, impotence or non-existence. Therefore, there is nothing among them as an instance of the meaning of existence in itself, and the Necessary Being is pure and the most complete Being. It has no limit [or definition] and no end and nothing else is mixed with it such as generality or specificity. Nor [is It mixed with] an attribute other than existence, in contrast with that which is other than It.

So we say: If the reality of existence did not exist, nothing would have been existent, because that which is other than the reality of existence is either an essence and is known to be non-existent in respect of its essence, or it is an imperfect and incomplete existence. Therefore, composition and specification will certainly be required at a determined level and specific limit of existence in the absolute sense. Therefore, it necessarily needs a cause to complete its existence, and a definiens [a defining term] to define it specifically and to bring it out of potentiality into actuality and out of contingency into necessity. This is because whatever reality (haqiqah) is not of existence is not required by its essence to have existence, nor does its selfhood require a specific degree of existence. So it will need something to overpower it and to limit it and to give it a determined level of existence and this requirement should be prior in existence to everything: the priority of the simple over the compound, the one over the many, the complete over the incomplete, the rich over the poor and the emanating source over the emanated.'[16]

An Explanation of the Version

This version is similar to the arguments of the 'urafa (gnostics), and thus it is as problematic as their arguments are. Furthermore, these words of Mulla Sadra, '...there is nothing among them as an instance of the meaning of existence in itself...' is also problematic. The existents in their totality are the instances of the concept of existence, and there is no difference between them in terms of conceptual instantiation. Their distinction lies in their external existence. The contingent existents are not expelled from the domain of existentiality in spite of being mixed with deficiency.

It is worth noting that the argument of the Sincere as advanced by Mulla Sadra in the *Asfar* is very close to the ontological argument of Shaykh al-Ishraq Suhrawardi as follows:

> 'If an incorporeal light is indigent with respect to its essence, [it does not mean that] it is in need of a lifeless obscure substance, because an obscure substance does not deserve creating that which is nobler and more perfect than it in every respect, and how can an obscure substance give light? So if an incorporeal light is in need of a self-subsistent light for its actualisation, then the series of the self-subsistent lights arranged in successive order will not regress ad infinitum, because you have come to know from the demonstration for the necessity of an end of an ordered coexistent series. Therefore, the subsistent and accidental lights, the barriers and the states must terminate in a light beyond which there is no light and it is the Light of Lights.'[17]

The main difference between the two arguments is that in Suhrawardi's argument, the impossibility of an infinite series has been employed as one of its premises, while in Mulla Sadra's argument, there is no need for this premise, though there might be some other differences.

Allamah Tabataba'i's Argument

Allamah Tabataba'i has propounded the argument of the truthful without using the premises used in the other versions. In this version, there is no need even for the fundamentality of existence. Thus, it can be considered an original version of the ontological argument in Islamic metaphysics.

In his gloss upon these words of Mulla Sadra, "As has been said, existence is a single simple objective reality", Allamah Tabataba'i writes:

> 'And this [objective reality] is the reality through which we reject sophistry and find that every sensible person is compelled to affirm it. It does not accept unreality or non-existence in itself; even supposing its unreality and non-existence necessitates its subsistence and existence. If we assume at a certain time or absolutely the unreality of whatever is real, and then if all reality really becomes unreal, it means that reality subsists. Likewise, if the sophist sees things as illusory or doubts their reality, they are really illusory and their reality is really dubious for him. It means that the negation of reality entails its affirmation. If the principle of reality does not admit non-existence and unreality by itself, then it is necessary by itself. Therefore, there is an essentially necessary reality, and the things that are real are in need of it and their reality subsists through it.'[18]

At this point, it becomes clear to those who reflect deeply that the reality of the essentially Necessary Being is necessary for man, and the arguments for His Existence are in fact [used] for drawing their attention [to It].

Another Version of Allamah Tabataba'i's Argument

Allamah Tabatab'i expounds the above-mentioned argument elsewhere as follows:

> 'The reality of existence about whose subsistence there is no doubt, never admits negation and non-existence. In other words, the reality of existence is unconditionally the reality of existence and does not become unreal unconditionally. As the universe is transient and each of its parts is susceptible to non-existence [obliteration], it is not the same as that very reality that does not admit negation but rather through that very reality it comes to possess reality and without it, it has no share of existence and is non-existent. Of course, it is not in the sense that reality should be united with things nor should it become incarnated in them nor should parts of reality be separated from it and join things but rather [it is] like light through which dark bodies become luminous and without which they are dark, and at the same time, this very example of light is not adequate to convey our purpose. In other words, It itself is the very reality, and the universe and its parts become real through It and without It they become null and void. The conclusion is that the universe and its parts, in terms of their existential independence and reality, depend upon a reality, which is the very same reality and which is the Reality by-itself.'[19]

This version has certain features:

1. It is not dependent upon any philosophical premises, that is, neither upon the premises of Mulla Sadra's argument nor even upon the premise of the argument of Sabzawari about the

fundamentality of existence. Thus, it can be said that it has an original importance because it needs no philosophical or other premises, and for this reason, it can be considered the most succinct and, if assumed to be complete, the most solid of arguments.

2. This argument proves the unity of the Necessary Being as well as proving the existence of the Necessary Being, because with respect to Its essential absoluteness and infinitude, there will be no possibility of assuming a partner. If the reality of everything depends upon it, and if it itself is the very same Reality, no partner can be assumed.

Conclusion

Ibn Sina's ontological argument has been espoused by most philosophers and theologians (*mutakallimūn*) following him. Though, it is preferable to the other arguments formulated before him, it rests upon a number of premises which seem to be more than enough. For this reason, Mulla Sadra sought to make the argument shorter and formulated another version of it. Thus, he offered a new version, which he regarded as an instance of the path of the sincere. In this argument, he does not use quiddity, quidditive or whatish contingency, motion or temporal beginning. He based his version upon the reality of existence and its specific properties and upon such philosophical principles as the principality, simplicity and gradation of existence.

After him, some other Muslim philosophers, such as Hajji Mulla Hadi Sabziwari, sought to reduce some of its premises. However, the version as expounded by Allamah Tabataba'i first elucidates the absoluteness of the Essence and then proves its necessity by relying on eternal necessity. This means the unconditional affirmation of the predicate of the subject in the light of the absoluteness and infinitude of the Real, its other attributes such as unity, knowledge, and the like can be dealt with one after the other.

Endnotes

1. Anselm, St., *Anselm's Basic Writings*, translated by S.W. Deane, 2nd Ed. (La Salle, IL: Open Court Publishing Co., 1962)

2. *Ibid.*

3. *Dua` al-Sabah* (The Supplication for the Morning): From `Abbas Qummi, *Mafatih al-jinan* with Persian Translation by Ilahi Qumshi'i , ed. by Sayyid Sadiq Mir Shafi`i, Quds edition, Tehran, 1383/2004, p. 121

4. Imam Ali, *The Nahj al-balaghah* (The Peak of Eloquence) with Persian Translation by Abd al-Muhammad Ayati, Tehran, Bunyad-i Nahj al-balaghah, 1376.

5. *Ibid.*

6. *Ibid.*

7. Al-Husayn, Prayer for the Day of `Arafah: From `Abbas Qummi, *Mafatih al-jinan* with Persian Translation by Ilahi Qumshi'i , ed. by Sayyid Sadiq Mir Shafi`i, Quds edition, Tehran, 1383/2004, pp. 551-552

8. *Sharh-i Ghur al-Fara'id or Sharh-i Manzumah*

Part one: Metaphysics, Arabic text and commentaries, edited with English and Persian introduction and Arabic-English glossary by M. Mohaghegh and T. Izutsu, Tehran, 1969, Second Edition 1981, p.3.

9. Shabistari, Mahmud, *Gulshan-i Raz, The Mystic Rose Garden, the Persian Text with an English Translation and notes chiefly from the Commentary of Muhammad ibn Yahya Lahiji.* Translated by E. H. Whinfield. Reprint of th1880 London edition ed. Lahore: Islamic Book Foundation, 1078, pp. 9-10.

10. Muammad Lahiji, *Mafatih al-i`jaz fi sharh-i Gulshan-i Raz*, edited by K. Sami`i (Tehran 1337 A. Hsh./ 1958), p. 69

11. Ibn Sina (Avicenna) *Kitab al-isharat wa al-tanbihat*, ed. Sulayman Dunya, Cairo, Dar al-Ma'arif, 1957-1968), Vol. 3, pp. 54-55.

12. *Kitab al-mash`ir (Le Livre des Penetrrations Metaphysiques)* edited and translated by Henry Corbin (Tehran/Paris 1064), pp. 67-68.

13. Shirazi, Sadra al-Din Muhammad, (Mulla Sadra) *al-Hikmah al-muta`alliyah fi al-asfar al-`aqliyyah al-arba`ah(The Transcendent Theosophy concerning the Four Intellectual Journeys of the Soul)*,Vol. 6, Ed. Muhammad Rida al-Mudaffar, Beirut, Dar al-Ihya wa'l-Turath, 1410 A.H./1990A.D., pp. 12-16

14. Sabzavari, Hajji Mulla Hadi, *Sharh-i Manzumah*. Trans. M. Mohaghaeh & T. Izutsu, *The Metaphysics of Sabzavari*, Tehran, Iran University Press, 1983, p. 32

15. Ha'iri Yazdi, Mehdi, *Hiram-i Hasti (The Pyramid of Existence)*, Second Edition, Tehran, Cultural Studies and Research Institute, 1983, pp. 40-47

16. Sadr al-Din Shirazi, *Asrar al-ayat(Secrets of the Verses of the Qur'an)*, ed. Muhammad Khajavi (Tehran: Iranian Academy of Philosophy, 1981), pp. 25-26.

17. Shihab al-Din Yahya Suhrawardi, *Majmu'ah musannafat Shaykh Ishraq*, ed. Henry Corbin (Tehran: Iranian Academy of Philosophy, 1977) Vol. 2, p. 121.

18. Tabataba'i ,`Allamah Sayyid Muhammad Husayn, Commentary on *al-Hikmah al-muta`alliyah fi al-asfar al-`aqliyyah al-arba`a*, Tehran, *Dar al-ma`arif*, 1950, Vol. 6, p. 14

19. Tabataba'i, `Allamah Sayyid Muhammad Husayn, *Usul-i falsafah wa rawish-i ria'lism* (*The Principles of Philosophy and the Method of Realism*) with an Introduction and Footnotes by Murtada Mutahhari, Qum, Sadra Publications, Vol. 5, 1375, pp. 116-117

20. It is worth noting that in the Qur'an, reference is made to the *siddiqin* in the verse: ``Those who have faith in Allah and His apostles - it is they who are the truthful and the witnesses with their Lord; they shall have their reward and their light'' (57: 19).

21. As for Sadr al-Din Shirazi (Mulla Sadra) see, for example, Seyyed Hossein Nasr, *Sadr al-Din Shirazi and His Transcendent Theosophy*, Tehran: Iranian Academy of Philosophy, 1978, and Fazlur Rahman, *The Philosophy of Mulla Sadra*, Albany: State University of New York Press (SUNY) , 1975.

Divine Justice

Mirza Abbas

This article looks at the phenomenon of divine justice: how it is addressed within the Islamic society, history and sciences, along with a brief introduction to certain authentic sources on the subject. It familiarizes the reader with the terminologies and principles that Muslim scholars use to explain and establish divine justice. The paper ends with the complete lesson on divine justice (*'adl*) by Ayatollah Misbāh Yazdī (b. 1934) from *The Theological Instructions*.

What is the Place of Justice within the Islamic Society?

Islam for Muslims is a religion that shapes man's personal and also social life. It provides the Muslims with a view and a yardstick through which they harmonize and organize their lives. The programme through which this is carried out is the *shari'ah* or Islamic law, which is based on justice. Hence, the phenomenon of 'justice' becomes central to Islam in the same way as shari'ah is central to Islam. A Muslim lives his life according to the shari'ah and this means that he is executing whatever is 'just' towards him and also towards the others. Justice encompasses his social and personal behaviour.

> 'It is a universal duty for everyone to implement justice both in his individual and social life. A Muslim is one who is just to himself, to his spouse and children, and to everybody else, including one's enemies.'[1]

Furthermore, according to the Shi'ite Islam, justice is considered as one of the five principal doctrines of faith or what is known as *"Usul al-Din"* (Principles of Religion). This demonstrates the crucial role that the concept of justice plays in knowing God and

133

the universe. However, divine justice has somehow always been a controversial topic within Islam and especially in theology. It is true that all Muslims believe that God is just but the complexity is how divine justice is understood or defined and what its reality is.

When Did the Discussions on Divine Justice Start?

The discussions on divine justice started soon after the advent of Islam in the seventh century under the category of *jabr* (predestination) and *ikhtīyār* (free will). Ayatollah Mutahhari asserts in this regard:

> '...the issue of predestination *(jabr)* and free will *(ikhtīyār)*, and that of divine justice, became current among Muslims during the first half of the second century of Hijrah. Perhaps the first formal centre of such discussions was the circle of al-Hasan al-Basri.'[2]

Nevertheless, there never existed an independent discussion or treatise on *'adl* in the early centuries (Mutahhari, 1999, p.17). Gradually the topic received more attention and independent works or chapters in books have been written on the subject, such as the *Divine Justice* by Ayatollah Mutahhari, *Al-Ilahiyyat* by Ayatollah Subhani, *Aqa'id-e Islami* by Ayatollah Makarem Shirazi and *Amuzesh-e Aqa'id* (Theological Instructions) by Ayatollah Misbah Yazdi, whose chapter on divine justice has been translated below. This is in addition to the contemporary exegeses of the Qur'an, which have adopted a thematic approach *(tafsir madu'i)* and dealt with the issue of justice as an independent theme, such as *Payam-e Qur'an* by Ayatollah Makārim Shirazī (b. 1929) or *Manshur-e Javīd* by Ayatollah Ja'far Subhānī (b. 1926).

Traditionally, when the discussions on justice are classified, one would come to the understanding that there have been three major schools of thought, which have had distinctive attitudes towards this issue. These are the Ash'arites, the Mu'tazilites, and the

Shi'ites.[3] Almost all of these schools seem to have categorized the discussions on justice into the topics of intrinsic goodness and badness (*al-husn wa al-qubh al-'dhati*), free will (*al-ikhtīyar*), divine decree (*al-qada wa al-qadar*), promise and threat (*al-wa'd wa al-wa'id*) and *bada*.

One must realise that research and the style of exercising the discussions on divine justice with the above-mentioned sub-headings within the Islamic seminaries can be divided into two types: intellectual ('*aqlī*) and traditional (*naqlī*). The former involves proofs and arguments on the basis of logic and intellect and the latter involves mainly reference to the scriptures. Traditional works such as *Bāb-e Hadī 'Ashr* by Allamah Hillī (d. 1307) and its well-known commentary by Shaykh Fazil Miqdad, *Tajrid al-I'tiqad* by Nasir al-Din Tusi (d. 1274) and its commentary, that is, *Kashf al-Murād* by Allamah Hilli along with modern works such as *Amuuzesh-e Aqa'id* by Ayatollah Misbāh Yazdī (b. 1934) and *Al-Ilahiyat* by Ayatollah Subhānī (b. 1926) are the main text books on this topic which are presently taught in the Shi'ite seminaries and more or less represent a synthetic approach.

What is the Meaning of Justice?

As this article investigates the way Muslim scholars have approached the issue of justice, it is necessary to know first what is meant by "justice". The lexical and the well-known meaning of justice is 'to place a thing in its proper place'. For example shoes, no matter how expensive they might be, belong to the feet and not to the head. Furthermore, other meanings such as fulfilment of rights towards others, consideration of one's potential and also purification of one's soul also fall under the category of justice.[4]

It should be noted that in the Qur'an, justice is used in relation to human acts and not God. In respect to God, emphasis has been put on the 'negation of injustice'.[5] Therefore, Muslim theologians and exegetes normally explain divine justice by saying, "God does not do injustice or break His promises".

Different Concepts Involved in Understanding Divine Justice

As indicated earlier, there are certain concepts that are discussed in theology in order to describe or prove divine justice. We will briefly consider these below.

Intellectual goodness and badness: It has been suggested that the issue of intellectual goodness and badness is the most important issue related to divine justice. In his commentary on *Kashf al-Murād*, Shaykh Ali Muhammadi Khurāsānī writes:

> 'The first issue under the topic of *'adl* is the issue of intellectual goodness and badness, upon which many other important concepts depend, such as divine wisdom, free will, pre-destination, and religious responsibility (*taklīf*). One who accepts intellectual goodness and badness will be able to understand freedom of choice and religious responsibility. However, one who rejects it will accept pre-destination.'[6]

In order to have a sound understanding of this concept, it is necessary to briefly point out the meaning of *'aql* and its authority (*al-hujjiyyah*).[7] According to the Ash'arites, intellect has no power to distinguish between what is good and what is bad or to understand what is good and what is bad. Whatever is commanded by God and is known in religion is good and whatsoever is prohibited by God, is bad. Furthermore, they also believe that whatever God carries out is good, even if it is punishing an innocent. However, the Mu'tazilites believed that goodness and badness are real and objective and that intellect has power to discern what is good and what is bad. Divine acts are known to be good, not just by definition. God performs what is really good and never does what is really bad. This belief is unlike that of the Ash'arites, "who saw good and bad as relative entities which adapted themselves to the conditions of time and space and were influenced by customs and indoctrinations".[8]

Ayatollah Jawādī Amulī (b. 1933), an eminent contemporary scholar, divides the discussion on goodness and badness into the following:

1. Are goodness and badness intrinsic or essential to all things?
2. If so, is there any way to understand their reality by our intellect?
3. If it is established that the intellect can understand them, is it restricted to understanding them just from a social point of view as praiseworthy or blameworthy, or can the intellect have its say in respect to the reward and punishment in the hereafter as well?

He asserts that as it was impossible for the Ash'arites to deny goodness and badness of a thing, they accepted the intellectual goodness and badness from a social point of view without having any influence in the hereafter. In other words, intellect can discern good and bad actions in social issues, but it cannot intervene in any theological or jurisprudential matters. On the other hand, the advocates of intellect, including the Shi'ites, have had the view that the intellect can not only discern the good and bad but can also have its say in respect to religious issues, even if there is no evidence available from hadith. For example, dishonesty of trust is bad and a dishonest deserves punishment in the hereafter. This understanding is an exercise of the intellect, hence becoming a religiously valid proof for the religion. In a similar manner, we can rationally understand that if something is obligatory its prerequisites are also obligatory.[9]

Amulī states three reasons for believing in *husn wa qubh:*

1. The testimony of conscience: Focusing upon his conscious, man can understand the phenomena of

beauty, ugliness, and of certain actions being corrupt and wrong without any influence or evidence from the scriptures. He will praise good actions like justice and kindness and condemn oppression and dishonesty and this tendency of his is regardless of his race, class, and religion and is due to the universal nature of the intellect.

2. Denial of intellectual goodness and badness leads to the denial of religion. If goodness and badness are only defined through the prophet and people cannot have an independent judgement about them, the possibility remains that the prophet himself may be telling lies. The only way to refute such possibility is to believe in intellectual goodness and badness.

3. The impossibility of verification of the religion, if intellectual goodness and badness are denied. If we reject the intellectual goodness and badness we will face a problem in respect to Prophethood and law because certainly the intellect judges that God is remote from any evil actions and therefore, there is no way to think that God may mislead us by giving miraculous power to false prophets or liars. Hence the intellect concludes that the prophets must be trustworthy and truthful individuals.[10]

This illustrates how essential the theory of intellectual goodness and badness is to argue for divine justice and for prophethood and imamate.

Promise and threat: Another issue related to divine justice is the issue of promise (of reward) and threat (of punishment). In some way or another, this issue is related to the issue of intellectual goodness and badness. The Mu'tazilites believe that our intellect tells us that breaking one's promise is bad and therefore whatever God has promised He will fulfil. On the other hand, the Ash'arites who deny reality of goodness and badness believe that God can act against His word. In other words, the Mu'tazilites emphasise that God will not break His own promises or forego His threats unless the servant repents. In this regard, Ayatollah Mutahari writes:

> '...the Mu'tazilite beliefs regarding divine retribution and divine forgiveness are interrelated, and both arise from their belief in inherent good and evil of deeds determinable by reason.'[11]

The Ash'arites emphasise that, if God desires to put Pharaoh into the heaven, He could, although he did not pay any heed to the guidance provided through Moses. This act of God is not against justice but a Mu'tazilite response to this could be that it is impossible for God to do so because this will be against justice as He has promised punishment for those who deny the truth.

Free-will and predestination: It has been suggested (Mutahari, 2004, p. 6) that one of the earliest debates within the Islamic society and among the scholars of Islam has been the debate on free will and predestination. Abu al-Hasan Ashari asserts, "all actions are due to the power of God and there is no action from the servant". In contrast, the Mu'tazilites assert, "certainly action executed by man is in the power of man and he has full control over them". This led to a major difference in understanding divine justice. However, the Shi'ites came up with the theory of 'the status between two statuses' (*amrun bayn al-amrayn*). According to Ayatollah Khomeini:

> '...every possible being executes action but not independently... there exists no independent doer than God the Supreme and all other beings are nothing but the relation to God and their existence is essential poverty (*faqr-e dhātī*).'[12]

In an interview with one of the contemporary teachers of "Transcendental Philosophy" of Mulla Sadra (d. 1640) who studied with 'Allama Tabātabā'ī (d. 1981), Hujjat al Islām wa al Muslimīn Tahrirī, I asked him about free will and predestination. He replied as follows:

> Tahiri: "The will of God can be divided into two parts: legislative (*tashri'i*) and meta-physical (*takwinī*). The former refers to His commands and the latter relates to His encompassing power. Man is created as a free being. If he transgresses the command of God he has trespassed the legislative will of God with the essential quality which God has given him but he is still within the meta-physical will of God as every activity is by His power."

> Author: "So, if the man has been created that way (freedom being in its essence) then his actions are independent in the like manner of a watch where the hands move clockwise as they are made that way?"

> Tahrirī: "No, the example is not right. In a watch the maker has no control, although he has made the watch to rotate, (in other words, rotation is in the essence of the watch) but in the case of man, God is constantly involved with His creation. He is constantly emanating grace through which the creation is existing."[13]

The assertion of Tahrirī also indicates 'the creed of middle position'; it is neither free will of man in total or predestination but it is something in between. Thereby the punishment on the day of judgement is justified and there remains room for the scholars to prove divine justice.

In order to understand the issue of *'adl* through a contemporary approach, in what follows, we will read the discussion on divine justice from *Amūzish-e Aqā'id* by Ayatollah Misbāh Yazdī.[14] This book consists of sixty lessons and is considered to be a breakthrough in the Islamic seminaries of Qum in the field of theology. One of the novelties of this book is that it deals with modern topics in theology and tries to answer some of the arguments developed against Islamic Beliefs. These sixty lessons are divided into three volumes and the discussions tend to follow the typical pattern of the roots or principles of religion: unity of God, divine justice, prophethood, imamate and resurrection.

FURTHER DISCUSSION ON DIVINE JUSTICE

Introduction

One of the most fundamental differences between the Ash'arites and the Mu'tazilites evolved around the issue of divine justice and the Shi'ite understanding of this issue is in agreement with that of Mu'tazilites. They have been known as the *'adliyyah* vis-à-vis *ashā'irah*. This topic is of great importance in the field of theology, and is known to be the crux of the matter in theological issues and is even acknowledged as one of the principles of belief for the schools of Mu'tazilite and Shi'ite.

One must focus on the point, that the Ash'arites do not deny divine justice and do not consider God as being unjust or tyrannical (God forbid), due to clear and apparent verses that establish divine justice and deny any form of oppression from the Holy divine realm. However the discussion centres around this issue that the sole intellect without any explanation from divine law (the Book and the traditions) can standardise divine actions. Upon this basis it can demand the forbearance and accomplishment of divine actions. For example: Is it necessary for God the Supreme to take a believer to heaven and a polytheist to hell, or are these decisions based on revelation and cannot be applied by the sole-intellect?

The point of dispute is that very issue, which has been referred to as good and evil through the intellect (husn wa qubh 'aqli). The Ash'arites have denied this and instead came up with the idea that whatever God carries out in the transcendental realm (takwīn) is considered as good, and on the corporal realm, whatever God orders is considered as good, but not because it is good by itself.

However, the belief of the Mu'tazilites and the Shi'ites is that action without any subsistence from the corporal and transcendental world can be distinguished by God as good and evil (husn wa qubh), and the intellect has the capacity to understand good and evil to a certain extent. This understanding results in the belief that the Holy divine realm is remote from evil actions. However this is not in the sense that God is commanded or ordered, but means that the emanation of evil from God the Supreme is incompatible, and the emergence of any evil from God is impossible.

Obviously the intellectual investigation has provided the answers to the doubts raised by the Ash'arites with regards to good and evil. Nevertheless, the current work does not have the capacity to display them. Likewise it is possible that the Mu'tazilites have some inadequate patterns in their belief with respect to the good and evil, which shall be investigated in its place. But the overall belief of good and evil from the intellectual point of view is acknowledged by the Shi'ites and has been confirmed in the Book and the traditions and emphasised by the Infallible Imams (a).

From here on we will be explaining the parameters of the concept of justice and then demonstrate intellectual arguments in order to prove this attribute as an attribute of action for God the Supreme. Finally we will resolve some of the most important issues dealing with this topic.

The concept of justice

The lexical meaning of justice is equity, or to equalise, and is commonly known as the consideration of the rights of others. Hence the definition would be 'granting rights to one who deserves.' Therefore, initially one must conceive an existence, which enjoys right, and then the consideration of its right will be known as justice, and the violation of it will be regarded as tyranny. However, occasionally the concept of justice can be extended to mean 'the performance of work befittingly or to place all things in its proper place.'

According to the latter definition, justice is tantamount to wisdom and just work is wise work. Nevertheless, the determination of the 'right of the deserved-one' and what a 'proper place' is, involves a vast domain of words, which is usually discussed in the philosophy of ethics and in the philosophy of rights. Naturally, this work does not allow us to cover all these peripheries.

Every mindful person understands that if a person snatches a piece of bread from an orphan's hand without any reason or kills an innocent person for no reason, they have persecuted and oppressed, and therefore committed an evil act. Furthermore in contrast to this, if the snatched bread is taken from the tyrant and given back to the orphan, or the killer is punished, the action carried out would be considered to be wise and just. This is true even for someone who does not believe in the existence of God.
The secret behind this discernment and the force that determines the good and evil, and similar issues must be investigated within the different branches of philosophy.

It may be concluded that justice can be conceived from two concepts, which are considered as general and particular. Consideration for the rights of others, the wise performance of work and heeding to the rights of others are an extension to this.

Therefore, the factor that is not necessary for justice is uniformity or equalisation. For example, a just teacher is not the one who encourages or reprimands students equally, whether they are hard working or lazy. A true teacher is the one who nourishes the one who deserve the nourishment. Another example could be that of a righteous judge who distributes the property in a feud according to the one who is entitled to that property, but not equally.

Similarly, the requirement of divine justice and wisdom is not that the Creator creates His creation uniformly or equally. For example, He does not create humans with horns, wings, wool etc. The necessity of divine justice and wisdom is that the Creator creates the existence in such a way that it receives the utmost good and perfection and also in a way that it fulfils the ultimate goal. Moreover, the essence of divine justice and wisdom is that all human beings are responsible according to their capacity and are judged and rewarded with consideration of their free will.

a. The proofs for divine justice

We know that God the Supreme possesses the ultimate level of power and volition, and can perform any work, which is possible without being under the influence of any being. However, He will not perform everything which is possible for Him to perform, but will act only upon that which He has desired and willed.

We also know that God's will cannot be absurd or uncalculated. He desires only that which His impeccable attributes necessitate of Him. He will not create any being without that which is demanded from His ontological attributes. God the Supreme is absolute (pure) perfection and His Will is related towards the perfection and benevolence of the creation. If the necessity of existence is the origination of evil and the imperfections in the universe, then it is considered to be one of the consequences of quintessentiality.

However this consequential evil and imperfection is predominated by perfection and good, because it is coherent with the abundant good and perfection (or because abundant good and perfection is quintessential). The abundant good will overwhelms the evil, because God the Supreme is absolute perfection.

Hence the requirement for the divine attributes of perfection is that the universe is created in such a way that it receives the utmost perfection and good, and from here the attribute of wisdom for God the Supreme is proved.

On this very basis, divine Will is related to man's creation when the right conditions are possible and are the source of abundant good. One of the fundamental privileges of man is volition and free will, which without doubt is an ontological attribute. An existent that possesses this quality is considered to be more perfect compared to one who is deprived of it. However the requirement for being independent is the movement towards eternal perfection through good actions, which can also descend in the direction of eternal loss and misery through bad conduct. The aim of divine Will is the perfection of man, and this is not possible without free will. This provides the possibility of deterioration due to the effect of sensual desires (*hawa al-nafs*), which take form because of the influences of Satan. Subsequently, this deterioration is also associated with divine Will.

Selection with awareness requires the understanding of good and evil. Hence God the Supreme has ordained for man, that which is beneficial and prohibited for him that which will lead him towards deterioration and decline. In addition, the requirement for divine wisdom is that responsibility must be harmonious with the capability of the performer, because a responsibility that is impossible to perform is absurd.

Therefore, the initial element of justice (in this particular sense) means justice in the ordinance of responsibilities. This is proved by the reason that if God the Supreme ordains a responsibility beyond the capacity of his servants, then the performance of it would not be possible.

'Justice in judgment' for the servants will be proved by focusing upon the factor of reward or chastisement provided for the action performed according to their (deserving) credibility.

Finally, justice in granting rewards and chastisement will be established by focusing upon the final purpose of creation. Man has been created in order to reach perfection or imperfection - if God rewards regardless of their work, He has not carried out His purpose.

Thus, the reason for the justice of God the Supreme in the true meaning and in all aspects is that the essential attributes of Him cause actions that are wise and just. None of the unjust, absurd, or fatuous attributes are present (exist) in Him.

b. The resolution of certain doubts

1. How can diversity that exists in the creation, particularly in human beings, be harmonious with divine justice and wisdom?

The answer given is that the diversity in creation is existentially advantageous and necessary for the order of creation. It is consequential to the principle of 'cause and effect.' The assumption that creation must be alike is an immature idea and if we look further we will understand that this type of idea is akin to the idea of not creating. For example, if all human beings were only men or women, there would be no birth or reproduction, resulting in the end of the human race. If all creatures were human beings then there would be nothing to consume or sustain our needs. If animals and plants were all of a single colour, we would lose the benefits and spectacular beauties that we find in creation. Appearances of different phenomena in distinctive forms are the results of conditions and these conditions are because of the movement of matter. Nobody has the right to make an objection regarding them, before his/her birth in order that He should have given it another form, or different place, or time, implying that there could be space for questioning the divine justice.

2. If divine wisdom is the cause of life for the human beings, why does God destroy them?

The answer to this question is that firstly, the life and death of existents in this world are the outcome of the relationships of cause and effect, the principle of creation (*takwīn*) and also a necessary element of the order of creation. Secondly, if the living creatures do not die then the grounds for newer creation will not be there and the future generation will be deprived of God's bounties. Thirdly, if it is assumed that all human beings were to remain alive, the earth would rapidly become a small place to live upon, and the inhabitants would wish for death due to despair and hunger. Fourthly, the true purpose for the creation of man is that he attains eternal felicity. If they do not transfer from this world through the medium of death they will not reach this final goal.

3. How can the existence of suffering and natural disasters (such as earthquakes, storms, etc) and other sociological hardships (such as war, oppression, etc) be harmonious with divine justice?

The answer to this question is that natural disasters are a requirement of action and reactions of matter. As good overwhelms evil, divine wisdom will not be contradicted. The eruption of sociological hardships and corruption in the world is due to the fact that humans are free in their action. Having a free will is the requirement of divine wisdom and the welfare for the society is more than that of corruption. If it were not the case then there would not exist a single man on the face of the planet. Secondly, the existence of all suffering and difficulty leads man to explore and search for the hidden natural sources and results in the appearance of sciences and different discoveries. Moreover, dealing with these difficulties will improve man's potential for advancement towards perfection. Nevertheless, if suffering is acknowledged in the proper sense then there will be a greater reward in the eternal world, and compensation will be given appropriately.

4. If eternal chastisement is intended for limited sins committed in this world, then how is it compatible with divine justice?

The reply to this question is that between the deeds and corresponding reward or punishment there is a relation of 'causation,' which has been disclosed to people through divine revelation. Likewise, some of the persecutions in this world have endurable consequences such as to blind oneself or others, which can take place in an instant but the result of this remains till the end of one's life. Similarly, great sins also have eternal effects and if a person does not arrange the means of atonement in this world (through seeking forgiveness) then the evil will remain with him forever. As with the case of blindness which will remain permanently due to an instant abuse, it does not contradict divine justice, eternal punishment for a great sin does not contradict divine justice also, because it is an action performed with full awareness.

Endnotes

1. Shomali, 2007, p. 30

2. d. 110/728-29

3. The Sunni majority have been mainly divided between the Ash'arites and the Mu'tazilites in the issue of *'adl*.

4. The reason why purification seems to come under the definition of justice could be due to the fact that it will be unjust towards the soul not to achieve purification after the opportunity provided.

5. See e.g. Shirāzī, 1371/1992, p. 403.

6. Muhammadi Khurāsānī, 1378/1999, p.200

7. Amuli, 1381/2002, p. 140

8. Mutahharī, 2004, p. 9

9. Amulī, 1381/2002, p. 141 – 46

10. Amulī, ibid, pp. 151-2

11. Mutahharī 1378/1999, p. 39

12. Khomeini, 1378/1999, p. 59

13. Tahiri, 2007

14. This book has been translated into English by the author and will soon be published by the title, *Theological Instructions*.

References

Amuli, Abdullah Jawādi (1381/2002), *Din Shenāsi,* Qum: Isra.

Kashāni, Mulla Muhsin Fayā (1407/1987) *Minhaj al-Nijāh,* Beirut: Dar al Islamiyyah.

Khomeini, Ruhullah Musawi. (1378/1999) *'Adl-e Ilāhi az Didgāh-e Imam Khomeini,* Qum: Mu'asseseh Tanzim wa Nashr-e Athār-e Imam Khomeini.

Muhammadi, Khurāsānī Ali. (1378/1999) *Sharh Kasf al-Murād,* Qum: Dar al-Fikr.

Mutahharī, Murtuza. (1378/1999), *'Adl-e Ilāhi,* Qum: Sadra.

(1378/1999), *Āshenā'i bā 'Ulúm-e Islāmi,* Qum: Sadra.

(2004), *Divine Justice,* trans. Sulayman Hasan Abidi, Murtuad'a, Alidina, Shuja 'Ali Mirza, Qum: International Centre for Islamic studies.

Shirāzī, Makārim. (1371/1992) *Payam-e Qur'an,* Qum: Madrese-ye Imam Amir Al-Mu'minin.

Shomali, M. A. (2007) *Islam: Doctrines, Practices & Morals,* London: Institute of Islamic Studies, Islamic Centre England.

Subhānī, Ja'far. (2006) *Introduction to the Science of Tafsir of the Qur'an* trans. Saleem Bhimji United Kingdom: Islamic Education Board of World Federation of KSIMC.

(1363/1985) *Manshú-e Jāwid,* Qum: Jāmi'yah Mudarresin.

Tahrirī, Muhammad Baqir. (2007), *Approaches of Muslim Scholars to 'Adl,* interviewed by the author, Mirza M Abbas Raza, transcript 19 September.

Yazdī, Muhammad Taqī Misbāh (1996), *Amúzish-e Aqā'id,* Qum: Sazemān Tablighat.